If You're Going the Wrong Way
... Turn Around!

James W. Moore

If You're Going the Wrong Way

...Turn Around!

How to Head in God's Direction

DIMENSIONS
FOR LIVING

NASHVILLE

IF YOU'RE GOING THE WRONG WAY . . . TURN AROUND!
HOW TO HEAD IN GOD'S DIRECTION

Copyright © 2004 by Dimensions for Living

This book is printed on acid-free paper.

Library of Congress Cataloging-in-Publication Data

Moore, James W. (James Wendell), 1938–
    If you're going the wrong way . . . turn around! : how to head in God's direction / James W. Moore.
        p. cm.
    ISBN 0-687-00688-0 (pbk. : alk. paper)
    1. Christian life—Methodist authors. I. Title.
    BV4501.3.M664 2004
248.4—dc22
                            2004010228

Scripture quotations, unless otherwise noted, are from the *New Revised Standard Version of the Bible,* copyright © 1989, by the Division of Christian Education of the National Council of the Churches of Christ in the United States of America. Used by permission. All rights reserved.

Scripture quotations marked RSV are from the *Revised Standard Version of the Bible,* copyright 1946, 1952, 1971 by the Division of Christian Education of the National Council of the Churches of Christ in the United States of America. Used by permission. All rights reserved.

Scripture quotations marked KJV are from the King James or Authorized Version of the Bible.

06 07 08 09 10 11 12 13—10 9 8 7 6 5 4 3

MANUFACTURED IN THE UNITED STATES OF AMERICA

IN HONOR OF JUNE AND HER COURAGEOUS SPIRIT

Contents

Introduction

If You're Going the Wrong Way . . .
Turn Around!
"How to Head in God's Direction"

Recently I attended a meeting that was held in the Worthington Hotel in downtown Fort Worth, Texas. As I checked out of the hotel, I asked the desk clerk, "What is the best way to get out of downtown Fort Worth and back to the interstate highway?" The clerk said, "That's easy. We are at the corner of Houston Avenue and Second Street. You will come out of the parking garage onto Houston Avenue. Turn right on Houston, go down to 6th Street and turn left, and it will take you right to I-35."

I did exactly what he said. I came out of the parking garage, turned right on Houston, went down four blocks to 6th Street, and turned left, and sure enough, I could see I-35 just ahead of me. I headed straight toward it. I drove just a short way and saw a ramp connected to I-35. I went up the ramp, rounded a curve, and you wouldn't believe what I saw. The ramp had three lanes, and painted on the three lanes were three bold arrows—and all three of those arrows were pointing straight at me! Quickly I realized that not only was I going the wrong way on a one-way street but, even worse, I was going *up* the off ramp of I-35, one of the busiest interstate highways in the world!

Well, I did what anyone in his or her right mind would have done: I made the fastest U-turn in the history of the world. A. J. Foyt, Jeff Gordon, and Mario Andretti would have been proud of that U-turn. I found out later that the hotel desk clerk had meant to say "5th Street" rather than "6th Street." But the point is clear. When you are going the wrong way, when you are going a dangerous way, a destructive way, a potentially deadly way, there is only one thing to do: Turn around as fast as you can!

This is true not only on the streets and highways of America. It also is true on the spiritual and moral roads of life. And the good news is this: With God, turnarounds are allowed! God permits turnarounds! God enables and empowers turnarounds! There are some situations in life that call for a turnaround; nothing else will work. Let me show you what I mean.

Suppose a man who works at the bank tells you that he has been stealing money from the bank. He tells you that he is taking home a thousand dollars a week of the bank's money and covering it up with creative bookkeeping. He tells you that he feels bad about what he has been doing and wants to stop. What would you say to that man? Would you say, "Well, why don't you cut back to $500 per week? Just take $500 per week home for several months, and then cut back to $250, and then to $100. Just taper off until you are not stealing anything at all." Is that what you would say to that man? Of course not! Absolutely not! You would tell him to stop that right now. You would tell him he is going the wrong way and he needs to make a turn-around with his life immediately. You would tell him what the Scriptures say about this: "Let him that stole steal no more" (Ephesians 4:28 KJV).

Or what if a man came to you and said, "I get drunk every Friday night, and then I go home and scream obscenities at my wife and children, and I really feel bad about that, and I really want to change." What would you say to that man? Would you say, "Well why don't you cut back a little bit and just get drunk once a month? Wouldn't that be refreshing to your wife and children, to go a whole month and not have you screaming obscenities at them? And then cut back to once a quarter, and later, only at Christmas and New Year's." Is that what you would say to that man? Of course not! Absolutely not! You would say, "Man, you need help. Let me take you to the church or to Alcoholics Anonymous. You have to stop this right now. You can't taper off. You've got to make a turnaround right now."

This is what the great biblical word *repent* means. It means, "Turn around. You are going the wrong way—a destructive, dangerous, deadly way." "Don't go that way anymore." Interestingly, the Hebrew word for "repent" is *hashivenu*. It is the same word used in the military for the command, "About face."

In the Gospel of Mark, when Jesus came out to start his ministry, this was the first thing he said: "The time is fulfilled, and the kingdom of God is at hand; repent, and believe in the gospel" (Mark 1:15 RSV). What Jesus was saying was this: "You have been going the wrong way; you have been going up the wrong road all this time. But now, have I got good news for you! I'm going to turn you around and show you a better way." Then Jesus went to the seashore. He saw Simon and Andrew and James and John in their fishing boats. Jesus was so perceptive. He saw the disillusionment, the despair, the look of defeat in their faces. And he said, "Come with me, and I will give you a new lease on life and a new sense of meaning. I want to take you up a new road and give you a new mission, a new joy, a new job, a new purpose." And look at what the Bible says here: Immediately—not gradually—*immediately* these men left their nets. They turned around and followed him (Mark 1:16-20, paraphrased).

Now if you and I will listen closely, Christ is speaking loud and clear to us. He is saying, "Let me turn your life around. Let me give you a new start. You don't have to go up all those wrong roads anymore. Let me show you a better way. Let me help you turn your life around." Now let me make this more specific with three thoughts.

First of All, If You Are Going Up the Road of Defeat, God Will Help You Turn Around

Have you heard the story about a shepherd who was out in his field keeping watch over his flock one afternoon? Suddenly a Jeep® Grand Cherokee pulled up. Out walked a young man in his twenties, dressed in khaki pants, a blue button-down shirt, and well-worn tennis shoes. The young man said to the shepherd, "If I guess how many sheep you have in your flock, will you give me one of them?" The shepherd said, "Okay." The young man pulled out his laptop computer, dialed into the Internet using a wireless connection, pulled up a GPS satellite site, located the area, and then a number of white dots representing the sheep came up on the screen. The young man quickly counted the dots and proudly told the shepherd that he had 1,586 sheep in his flock.

The shepherd was amazed. This was the correct number, so he told the young man to pick out a sheep. The young man picked one out, put it into his Jeep, and prepared to drive off. The shepherd said, "Before you leave, I have a challenge for you. If I guess your occupation, will you give me your Jeep?" The young man agreed. The shepherd promptly told the young man that he was a consultant. The young man was shocked and amazed, and he asked the shepherd how on earth he figured that out. The shepherd said, "It was easy. First, you came without being called. Second, you charged me a sheep to tell me something I already knew. And third, you obviously don't know anything about what I do, because that was my dog you just put into your Jeep!" Talk about a turn! What looked like defeat for that shepherd suddenly became a victory.

Let me take that concept to a deeper level by telling you about Kim and Leslie Wheless. They inspired all of us who knew them with the beautiful way in which they loved and cared for each other, and the powerful way in which they lived their faith in a difficult situation. They had been married for fourteen-and-a-half years, and that entire time (and a little before) Leslie had been battling cancer. I lost count of the number of times she went into the hospital, the number of times she went through chemotherapy, the number of times she lost her hair, never once complaining, always smiling, always battling, always praying, and always beautiful—with Kim always at her side.

But then her body became more fragile, and then one Friday morning the phone rang in my office at 11:30, and through tears, Kim told me what I had been dreading to hear: "We just lost Leslie." I rushed to the hospital to help Kim do the things you have to do in that situation—call the family and friends, notify the funeral home, sign the papers, start making the arrangements, gather the person's belongings from the room, and leave the hospital, without Leslie. It was a hard thing to do. As Kim and I walked out of the hospital, the day was dark and dreary, but as we drove toward Kim's home, suddenly the sun came out, and it was shining gloriously. It overcame the dark and dreary clouds, and I said to Kim, "Leslie is there now, and heaven is brighter!"

It's a parable for us, isn't it? Death is not defeat for the Christian. Death is not the end at all for the Christian. It is simply a door we go through to reach a deeper level of existence with God. It may look like you are going up a road of defeat, when suddenly God turns it into a road of victory. On that first Good Friday, the disciples must have felt discouraged and defeated as they saw with their own eyes their master nailed to a cross, and yet God took that awful moment that looked like defeat and turned it into His greatest victory. Listen! If you feel like you are going up a road of defeat (whatever that may be for you), God can turn it around. God can help you turn around.

Second, If You Are Going Up the Road of Mixed-Up Priorities, God Will Help You Turn Around

Let me ask you something. Have you figured out yet what are the things in life that really matter—the things that really count, that really are important? Have you? Or are you still confused? Are you still going up the road of mixed-up priorities?

Dr. Fred Craddock tells a true story about a missionary family who had served in China for some time when suddenly one day Communist soldiers barged into their home and placed them under house arrest. They were held prisoner for sixty days. One morning, the soldiers abruptly came to the missionary, whose name was Glen, and told him and his wife that they would be released the next morning and flown to freedom but that they could only take 200 additional pounds with them. Now, they had been in China many years and had accumulated many things, so hard decisions would have to be made quickly.

They began to discuss what to take. Glen said, "Of course, we must take all of my books and sermons, and my new typewriter."

"Oh, Glen," said his wife, "your books weigh so much, and you don't need to take the typewriter! Besides I have these wonderful antique vases. They are so special. We must take them."

What started as a nice discussion soon became a full-scale heated argument. Each thought the other was being stubborn and selfish. Each was praying that God would bring the other to his or her senses. They went to bed that night in angry silence, neither willing to bend even a little or give an inch.

The next morning when the soldiers arrived with their scales, Glen elbowed in ahead of his wife and hurriedly placed his books and sermons and his typewriter on the scales. His wife stood to the side, hugging her antique vases and seething. The soldiers weighed Glen's things and said, "They weigh 200 pounds."

"That's what you said," answered Glen, "200 pounds."

"Yes, that's right," said the soldiers, "but how much do the children weigh?"

"You mean?"

"Yes! Yes!"

With tears of shame in his eyes, Glen laid aside his books and sermons and typewriter. He looked over to see his wife putting down the antique vases. Then they ran into each other's arms, holding each other tightly, hugging each other and saying, "How could we have been so foolish? God forgive us. God forgive us!" (adapted from *Craddock Stories* [St. Louis: Chalice, 2001], pp. 22-23).

Talk about a turnaround! Those words, "How much do the children weigh?" brought them back to their senses, back to each other, back to God, and back to the right priorities. Listen, if you are going up the road of defeat or up the road of mixed-up priorities, then you need to turn around and come back to the things that really matter. You can do it because God will help you.

7

Third and Finally, If You Are Going Up the Road of Sin, God Will Help You Turn Around

Sin means "separation from God." Anything we do or say or feel that separates us from God and from other people is sinful. Life is meant to be a journey that brings us closer and closer to God, and at any given moment we either are moving toward God or moving away from God. So let me ask you, how is it with you right now? Which way are you traveling? Are you going toward God or away from God?

As many in our church family know, our granddaughter Sarah says the most interesting things. When she was seven years old, her maternal grandmother, Dede, was visiting at Sarah's home in Plano. Dede and Sarah were in the kitchen early in the morning, and Dede was fixing breakfast when she asked Sarah this question: "Sarah, do you know where your mom keeps the toaster?" Sarah answered, "Dede, I don't know that much about the kitchen, but let me tell you what I do know about. I know about God, Jesus, my family, my friends, Albert Einstein, and Dr. Martin Luther King. Which one of those would you like to talk about?" She always has an answer.

Recently Sarah told my wife, June, and me a story she had learned in school, acting it out with dramatic flare. It was an old Native American legend about a boy who climbed to the top of a mountain to prove his manhood. He was very proud, but as he started back down the mountain, he heard a sound at his feet. It was a deadly snake. The snake spoke to him and said, "Please help me. I am about to die up here. It's too cold for me, and there is no food. Put me under your shirt and take me down to the warmth of the valley." "Oh, no," said the boy, "I know your kind. You are a rattlesnake. If I pick you up, you will bite me, and your poisonous bite will kill me!" "Not so," said the snake,

"I will treat you differently. If you do this for me, I will never harm you."

The young boy resisted for a while, but the snake was very persuasive. Finally, the young boy gave in. He picked up the snake, tucked it under his shirt, and carried it down to the warmth of the valley. There he gently laid it down. Suddenly the snake coiled, rattled, and struck, biting the boy on the leg. "But you promised!" cried the boy, "You promised!"

"You knew what I was when you picked me up," said the snake as it slithered away.

The point of Sarah's story is clear: There are some things in life we had better not pick up. They are dangerous because they take us away from God. We know what they are. I could rattle off a list of sins, but we all know what they are. That's not the problem. The problem is that we get duped like that young boy. The sins of our time are so persuasive, so enticing. They tell us they won't bite us, they won't hurt us, they will treat us differently; but don't you believe that for a minute. Don't buy that. Don't go that way. It's the wrong way. If you are going up the road of defeat, the road of mixed-up priorities, or the road of sin, then call out to God. God can save you. God can deliver you. God can help you turn your life around.

1

From Talking About the Cross to Taking Up the Cross

"IT'S NOT ENOUGH TO BE GREAT ON PAPER"

Read 1 Corinthians 12:27-31.

Recently I ran across a list of contemporary signs, signs on the doors of various businesses. Let me share some of these with you:

- On the door of a car dealership: "The best way to get back on your feet is to miss a car payment."
- On the door of a veterinarian's office: "Back in a few minutes. Sit! Stay!"
- On the door of a muffler shop: "No appointment necessary; we'll hear you coming."
- On the door of a computer store: "Out for a quick byte."
- On the door of a funeral home: "Drive carefully. We'll wait."
- On the door of a hospital maternity room: "Push, push, push."

- On the door of an eye doctor's office: "If you can't see what you're looking for, you've come to the right place."

Signs are an important part of life in our time, aren't they? In a different way, signs were an important part of life in biblical times. This was the challenge people repeatedly threw at Jesus. "Show us a sign." "Give us some dramatic signal." "Hit us with some exciting proof." "Wow us with a flashy miracle that will convince us without question that you really are the Son of God."

At first, Jesus met these demands with a deep sigh: "What more do you want me to do? You have seen my healing miracles. You have seen me feed the 5,000. You have seen me calm a storm. If you're not convinced by these signs, what sign will do it for you?"

But you remember, of course, that ultimately Jesus did give us another sign, the greatest sign of all: the sign of the cross! What a powerful, moving, eloquent sign that is! It's the dramatic symbol of unconditional love, unwavering forgiveness, amazing grace, unflinching commitment, sacrificial service. And then you remember when Jesus came off the cross and out of the tomb, he said to us: "Look at this, now. Here is how I want you to live. I want you to take up my cross and live in this spirit of unconditional love, unwavering forgiveness, amazing grace, unflinching commitment, and sacrificial service."

But you see, our problem too often is that we like to talk about the cross and sing about the cross but we are not really sure that we want to live like that. Let me show you what I mean with a couple of quick illustrations.

First, you know in the "Peanuts" comic strip that Lucy is madly in love with Schroeder, the musician, but she can't get his attention. He just sits on the floor and plays his toy piano with great intensity, and he absolutely ignores Lucy.

She tries and tries to turn his head and win his love, but to no avail. Schroeder ignores her.

Finally, Lucy says, "Schroeder, do you even know what love is?" Abruptly, Schroeder stops his piano playing, he stands to his feet, and says precisely: "Love: a verb, it means to be fond of, to value; it's to have a strong affection for or an attachment to or devotion to a person or persons." Then he sits back down and automatically resumes playing his piano. Lucy sits there, stunned for a moment, and then she says, sarcastically, "On paper, he's great!"

That was how Jesus felt about some of the religious leaders of his day: on paper, they were great! They looked pious. They sounded religious. They spoke high-sounding theological words into the air. They prayed feverishly. They rushed to the Temple constantly. But somehow, it never got translated into the way they dealt with people. They spoke of love but never got around to being loving. They were religious outwardly, but they didn't know how to help and heal and serve—they were great on paper. They were so heaven-bound that they were no earthly good!

Now, here's another illustration. One Friday afternoon, I was in the study working on a sermon on "Loving People." I was really into it. Thoughts were flowing, ideas were popping. It felt so right. And I thought, "This is going to be a masterpiece!" Just about then, the phone rang. Someone was calling to tell me that a homeless family had come to the church for help. They needed food and bus tickets to Birmingham, Alabama. No other ministers were around at the moment. Could I come and help them?

As I left the study to go meet with this family, I remember thinking rather impatiently, *Who are these people, anyway? Why are they disturbing me? Don't they realize that I'm creating a masterpiece sermon on* love *here?* Then it hit me, what I was doing, and I felt ashamed. For you see, I realized that talking a good game is not enough. Only when our creeds are translated into deeds are they worth anything.

Helping people is more important than *talking* about helping people. Loving people is more important than writing sermons about loving people. So I asked God to forgive me, and I went and helped that family and then came back to my sermon.

But the temptation is always there, isn't it? The temptation to forget that we, as Christians, are first and foremost servant people, the temptation to look good on paper but not to translate our creeds into deeds. That kind of religion was a real turnoff to Jesus. That's why he said, "You will know them by their fruits," in other words, by their acts of love, not by pious phrases or public displays of religiosity. "Not everyone who says to me, 'Lord, Lord,' will enter the kingdom," he said, but only those who in faith imitate God's loving ways (Matthew 7:21).

It is significant to note that so often in the parables of Jesus the key question asked is this: "How did you treat your neighbor?" That's what separates the sheep from the goats. Active love is the sign of discipleship. Active love is the emblem of faith. Active love is the key to the kingdom. That's what Jesus said repeatedly in the Sermon on the Mount. And in so doing, he sounded a dramatic warning. In effect, he said, "It's not enough just to talk a good game. It's not enough just to be religious." As Christians we are called to imitate his sacrificial love. We are called to be his servants, to live in his gracious, self-giving, helping, healing spirit, to accept his love in faith and then to pass it on to others.

Now, let me bring this closer to home and be more specific with three thoughts.

First of All, We Are Called to Be Servant People

We are always tempted to be selfish. We are even tempted to be religiously selfish, to cry *What's in it for me?* and to think only of saving our own skins, to see faith as nothing more than an insurance policy for another day.

Occasionally I see a bumper sticker that always troubles me. It says, "Warning! In Case of the Second Coming, This Car Will Be Left Driverless!" That bothers me. That kind of religious gloating is so holier-than-thou that it turns me off. "I've got something you don't have! Bully for me, and tough for you!" What kind of religion is that? It's not what Jesus had in mind. That kind of religious arrogance upset him and drew his strongest rebukes.

In 1977, *Guideposts* magazine reported a true story about a man hiking in the mountains. He was surprised by a sudden snowstorm and quickly lost his way. Since he was not dressed for the frigid weather, he knew that he needed to find shelter fast or he would freeze to death. Despite all his efforts, time slipped by, and his hands and feet became numb. He knew his time was short now. Then he literally tripped over another man who was almost frozen to death. The hiker had a hard decision to make. What should he do? Forget about the man and continue on, trying to save himself? Or should he try to help the stranger in the snow?

He started to walk on, but he couldn't do it. He came back and threw off his wet gloves. He knelt beside the man. He began to talk to him while massaging the stranger's arms and legs. Soon, the man in the snow began to respond, and together they were able to find help. The hiker was later told by the doctors that helping the man in the snow had saved his own life. For you see, the numbness, which had stricken him, had vanished while he was massaging the stranger's arms and legs.

This is what Jesus meant when he said that when we try to selfishly save our lives, we lose them, and when we lose our lives for others, that's when we get saved. So we need to beware of being so selfish that we miss the world of service.

Second, We Are Called to Be Gracious People

Some of the religious leaders in the time of Jesus were so narrow, so harsh, so rigid, so critical, so judgmental that they weren't very gracious, and that bothered Jesus. He spoke of this often. He urged us not to be so critical and harsh with one another but rather to live in the spirit of forgiveness and grace.

Some years ago, a friend of mine went through a painful experience. He and his teenage daughter had argued bitterly one Saturday night. Later that evening, the daughter stole some money from her parents and ran away. Her mom and dad were heartsick and worried about their daughter. Some days later they received word that someone had seen her in Galveston, Texas. They wrote a beautiful letter to their runaway daughter telling her of their deep concern for her, their unconditional love for her, and pleading with her to come home to their waiting arms—or at least to pick up the phone and call them collect. "If we could just hear your voice," they said, "we would cry for joy."

They made a hundred copies of the letter and then went to Galveston and posted the letter in every restaurant, every nightspot, every public place they could find in the hopes that she might see one of those letters and come home. That is exactly what happened. Over and over, in place after place, their daughter saw the letter. She was so touched by her parents' gracious love and forgiveness that she did come home, and what an incredible moment of reconciliation it was!

I don't know anything in this world more beautiful than the spirit of grace and the ministry of forgiveness. We need to beware of being so selfish and judgmental that we miss the world of grace. We are called to be servant people, and we are called to be gracious people.

Third and Finally, We Are Called to Be Committed People

Many of you may be familiar with the name of Dr. M. Scott Peck. He wrote the best-selling book *The Road Less Traveled*. In another of his books called *People of the Lie*, Scott Peck writes about one of his most difficult counseling situations, a woman he calls Charlene. At a crucial point in her counseling, right after she had complained that everything in life seemed meaningless, Dr. Peck asked her, "Well, what do you think the meaning of life is?" She refused to answer. So, Dr. Peck said to her, "What do you think is the purpose of human existence? You call yourself a Christian; how would a Christian answer that question?"

"We exist to serve God," Charlene said in a flat, low monotone, as if she were sullenly repeating an alien catechism, learned by rote and extracted from her at gunpoint. "The purpose of our life is to glorify and serve God," she said.

"Well," Dr. Peck responded. (That's the way therapists talk—"Well.") There was a short silence. For a brief moment, Scott Peck thought she was about to burst into tears. But then with a suddenness and a venom that startled Scott Peck, her choked-back sobs turned into a dramatic roar as she screamed, "I don't want to live for God! I don't want to serve him! I can't do it! I won't do it! I want to live for me! I want to do what serves me! I want to live for my own sake!" That's what Charlene said (*People of the Lie* [New York: Simon and Schuster, 1983], pp. 167-68).

Now, most of us would never say something like that out loud so blatantly, so graphically, so irreverently. But you know as well as I do, that we have our own little subtle ways of saying that. The poet expressed it like this:

> Yes, I'll go where you want me to go, Dear Lord,
> Real service is what I desire.

I'll say what you want me to say, Dear Lord,
But don't ask me to sing in the choir.

I'll say what you want me to say, Dear Lord,
I like to see things come to pass.
But don't ask me to teach girls and boys, Dear Lord,
I'd rather stay in my class.

I'll do what you want me to do, Dear Lord.
I'll yearn for the kingdom to thrive.
I'll give you my nickels and dimes, Dear Lord,
But, please don't ask me to tithe.

Yes, I'll go where you want me to go, Dear Lord,
I'll say what you want me to say.
But, I'm busy now with myself, Dear Lord,
I'll help you . . . but, some other day.

Listen closely, now: Don't put it off any longer! Don't procrastinate anymore! Don't make any more excuses! God has a job for you. God has a special task for you. God has a ministry for you. God has a unique place of service that only you can fill. If you will listen closely, you can hear him. You can hear him calling your name, and you can say with the hymn writer, "Here I am, Lord." I hear your call, so go with me, Lord, and help me to take up my cross and serve you well.

Here I am, Lord. Deliver me from selfishness. Enable me to turn my life around. Help me to be your *servant*. Help me to be *gracious*. Help me to be *committed* to you.

2

From Old Life to New Life

"SOME THINGS JUST NEED TO BE THROWN AWAY"

Read Matthew 5:30.

Let me remind you of something they do in a certain village in Italy on New Year's Eve. They don't dress up and go to a festive party. They don't sing "Auld Lang Syne." They don't gather in the town square and watch a glittering ball drop to announce the exact moment when the new year begins. No, they pretty much all stay home, and as midnight approaches, traffic on the streets begins to lessen. Soon there is no traffic at all. No cars. No pedestrians. Even the police take cover because they know what's about to happen.

Then, at the precise stroke of midnight, the windows of every house in the village open up, and to the sound of music, fireworks, and laughter, people with reckless abandon begin to throw things out the windows: worn-out furniture, chipped glasses, cracked dishes, clothes gone-out-of-style, old pots and pans no longer wanted, old shoes that no longer fit, pictures of old boyfriends or girlfriends, personal items that are reminders of difficult experiences in the past year. Out the window they go. All those things that the people do not want to carry with them into the new year go flying out the windows.

Actually, if you stop to think about it, the Italians in that little village have a great idea. Now, if you decide to try this, and especially if you live in a high-rise, you may want to warn your neighbors that you're starting a new custom, and you may want to get permission from city hall and your landlord.

The point of this unique village custom, however, is well taken because there are indeed times in our lives when we need to make a clean sweep of it. There are times in our lives when we need to stop and evaluate and throw out those things that are burdening us, hampering us, hurting us, and hurting those around us.

This is precisely what Jesus was talking about in the Sermon on the Mount when he said those words that at first hearing seem so harsh and shocking: "And if your right hand causes you to sin, cut it off and throw it away" (Matthew 5:30). "Cut it off and throw it away"? These words sound so strong, so stark, so startling. There must be some truth here that is tremendously important to prompt Jesus to speak so boldly and so unflinchingly. What are we to make of this?

Of course, we know that Jesus was speaking symbolically here. The actual literal cutting off of a hand was certainly not what Jesus had in mind at all. Jesus is speaking dramatically here, calling us to the discovery of a much deeper truth, namely this: If you have something in your life right now that is destructive, then cut it out and throw it away! Get rid of it before it destroys you.

If you are smoking and it's destroying your lungs, quit smoking! If you are drinking and you are becoming an alcoholic, quit drinking! If you are gambling and losing all of your food money at the track, quit gambling! Whatever you are doing that is bad for you and bad for those around you, cut it off, quit it, throw it out before it does you in.

Nowhere is this "cut it off and throw it away" principle truer than in our spiritual lives. There are certain acts, certain attitudes, certain habits, certain sins that will contaminate, infest, and poison our souls. Jesus knew that, and he knew that the only way we can be spiritually fit and spiritually whole is to get rid of them.

Now, let me list three things we would do well to cut out of our lives and throw away.

First of All, Throw Out Selfishness

If you read the Bible closely, you will discover that the real culprit in our spiritual lives is selfishness. And on the flip side of the coin, the height of spiritual maturity, according to the Scriptures, is love for God and love for others.

I had a seminary professor who put it strongly. He said there is really only one sin with a capital letter, with lots of little sins underneath. He said the big sin is the sin of idolatry—the worshiping of something other than God—and he said that something we most often put in front of God is "self." My professor went on to say that the sin of self-centeredness has many variations—such as pride and arrogance, immorality, prejudice, hatefulness, violence, stealing, hurting, and obscenity—but he said they all root back to selfishness. They all root back to putting self before God and before others.

This problem of selfishness is so threatening and so dangerous that Jesus used dramatic language to describe how we need to be converted from selfishness to love. He said, "We must be born again! We must die to selfishness before we can come alive to love." Bishop Kenneth Shamblin once said, "Conversion means moving from 'That belongs to me' to 'I belong to that'!"

The noted psychologist Alfred Adler once put an ad in the newspaper that read "Guaranteed: Fourteen-day cure for loneliness." A woman showed up at his office, ad in hand, and said, "It says here that you can cure my loneliness in fourteen days. Is that true?"

"Absolutely," said Dr. Adler. "If you will do exactly what I tell you to do for fourteen days, you won't be lonely anymore."

"Tell me more," said the woman.

Dr. Adler said, "For fourteen consecutive days, I want you to go out and do something kind for somebody else."

The woman said, "Why should I do something kind for somebody else?"

To which Dr. Adler replied, "In your case, it might take twenty-one days!" (Jane Nelsen, *Positive Discipline* [New York: Ballantine, 1996], pp. 23-24.)

When we live in the spirit of selfishness, we are likely to end up bitter and miserable or lonely. On the other hand, when we live as God meant for us to live, reaching out to others in the gracious, loving, thoughtful spirit of Christ, we will end up filled with a sense of meaning and purpose and joy and fulfillment.

An old Native American of the Cherokee tribe was telling his grandson about a battle that was going on inside himself, a battle between two wolves. One wolf was evil, representing anger, envy, greed, arrogance, self-pity, guilt, resentment, false pride, and ego. The other wolf was good, representing joy, peace, love, hope, humility, faith, benevolence, generosity, compassion, and kindness. The grandson thought about it for a minute and then asked his grandfather, "Which wolf won?" The old Cherokee simply replied, "The one I feed."

Precisely so. And this is why Jesus taught us in words and deeds to feed and nurture love and kindness in our lives. This is why he told us over and over again to "Get rid of selfishness! Cut selfishness out of your life! You don't need it anymore! Throw it away, cast it off! Throw it out!"

Second, Throw Out Defeat

The Scriptures boldly and confidently tell us that if we put our faith and trust in God and commit our lives to him, we can't be defeated. Of course we will have some setbacks in life. Of course we will have some disappointments. Of course we will have some heartache and sorrow and pain. But the bottom line is, God wins—ultimately God wins, and if we hang in there and count on God and trust in God, nothing, not even death, can defeat us. That is the great promise of the Bible.

Some years ago a young man named Bobby Burnette showed up on the campus at the University of Arkansas. He was there on a football scholarship. The coaches knew that he had been an outstanding running back in high school, yet early on, they got the impression that Bobby Burnette was a fast runner but that he didn't like to be hit. So they used him as a tackling dummy. The veteran players hit him and hit him and hit him, working on their tackling techniques. Bobby Burnette never complained. He just kept getting back up. He refused to quit.

For three and a half years, Bobby Burnette showed up for practice at the University of Arkansas, and he never dressed out for a game. Finally the coaches let him put on a uniform and stand on the sidelines. They had no intention of putting him in the game. He had been the tackling dummy for three and a half years and had never really had the chance to show what he could do in a football game.

But then that Saturday afternoon, the first-string tailback got hurt, and then the second-string tailback got hurt, and the coaches had no other choice, so reluctantly they sent Bobby Burnette into the game. On his first play in the game, they gave Bobby Burnette the ball. He went through the hole, ran right over the linebacker, and made an outstanding run. From that point on, he was Arkansas's starting tailback, and he became a big-time star.

In the Cotton Bowl that year, Bobby Burnette made the key play that put Arkansas in position to win the game. Two plays later, Bobby Burnette dove over the goal line, and Arkansas won the Cotton Bowl game 10 to 7, and the next day the Arkansas Razorbacks were proclaimed National Champions.

The next year, Bobby Burnette started every game, had a great season, made the All-Conference Team, and was drafted to play in the NFL—and his first year as a pro, he was named "Player of the Year." For three and a half years at Arkansas, he didn't even dress out for the games, but he would not quit, he would not give up, he would not accept defeat.

If you do a study of the great champions in sports and in all aspects of life, you will find that they all have one common quality. It's not speed. It's not talent. It's not size. It is *persistence.* They will not quit. They will not give up. They will not accept defeat. They persist. They persevere. This is also the quality of the spiritual champions. They know God ultimately will win, and so they hang in there with God. They keep on trusting God, come what may.

So, as we think about the things in our lives that we don't need anymore, a good place to start is by throwing out the spirit of selfishness and the spirit of defeat.

Third and Finally, Throw Out Ill Will

"Ill will" is a phrase that means a lot of things and covers a multitude of sins. Bad temper, hostility, vengeance, resentment, arrogance, spite, hatefulness—all of these are what we mean by "ill will," and ill will is a fitting name for all of these because they all are sick. Nothing is more spiritually poisonous than ill will.

Christ came to bring us wholeness, to make us well, to deliver us from all these sins of ill will. Again, this is what conversion is. It is Christ coming into our lives and changing our ill will to goodwill.

Have you heard about the man who was sitting in his car at a traffic light? He was second in line. When the light turned green, the car in front of him didn't proceed immediately, and the man in the second car went ballistic. He just lost it. He shouted expletives out the window. He honked his horn in a wild rage. He made obscene gestures toward the driver in front of him. Finally, the first car moved on through the intersection. The man in the second car made it through also, but he was still shouting and gesturing his profanities.

A police car pulled him over. The police officer got him out of the car, handcuffed him, searched him, and put him in the backseat of the squad car. The officer called headquarters, he talked for a few minutes, and then he helped the arrested man out of the backseat, took off the cuffs, and told the man he was free to go. The police officer said, "Well, surprise to me, it is your car after all! Sorry for the inconvenience. You are free to go." The baffled motorist asked, "What on earth was that all about?" "Well," said the police officer, "When I saw the bumper stickers on the car that read 'Honk if you love Jesus' and 'God loves you, and I love you,' and then I saw how you were acting, I just naturally assumed that you must have stolen that car."

Well, the point is clear: Ill will is not representative of who we are as Christians, and it is something we don't need to carry with us anymore. It's time. It's time to throw some things out the window of our lives. It's a good time to throw out selfishness, to throw out defeat, and to throw out ill will.

3

From the Quick Fix to the Deep Commitment

"Good Things That Are Here to Stay Don't Get Done in Just One Day"

──────────

Read Mark 10:17-22.

Some years ago, a famous senator from middle America was asked what was the single most difficult aspect of being a United States senator. His answer was interesting. He said the hardest thing to deal with in his job as a United States senator was the frustrating fact that his constituents back home had "a bad case of the simples." That is, they expected him to work instant miracles up in Washington. They so easily reduced all complexities to very neat little black-and-white simplicities. He said they didn't seem to realize that the most meaningful and significant accomplishments take time, effort, commitment, sacrifice, discipline, and perseverance.

In a sense, this was the rich young ruler's problem. When he came to Jesus in search of real life, in search of something to fill the inner emptiness gnawing at him, in search of something to satisfy that deep hunger in his soul, he wanted no complicated personal involvement. He wanted an easy answer, an instant miracle, a simple solution. But then when Jesus told him that this was no simple matter—that this is a life commitment that touches all that you have and all that you are—the rich young man turned away sorrowfully because he wanted a fast, easy, simple remedy, a quick fix.

Remember the story with me. Jesus has set his face toward Jerusalem. He is on his way to the Holy City, on his way to the cross. This is serious business, now. Jesus is thinking deep thoughts when the rich young ruler runs up and kneels before him and asks about eternal life.

There are some fascinating things to notice here. This man is rich, he is young, and he is a ruler. In other words, he has all the things that we in our world so openly long for: wealth, youth, and power. Some would say, "He has it made! He has it all! Wealth, youth, power—what more could he want?"

But you see, that is precisely the point. Despite having all those things, something is missing in his life. He knows it, he feels it, he senses it. Something is missing! There is a void, a vacuum, an emptiness, a hunger that is not satisfied, a thirst that is not quenched.

Money, power, and youthfulness, wonderful as they are, are not enough. Something more is needed to make his life full. The young man knows that his life is incomplete, so he comes to Jesus in search of a quick and simple solution. After all, he is probably used to getting exactly what he wants, simply and quickly. He is a ruler. When he speaks, people are quick to say, "Yes, sir." When he calls, people jump and come immediately. When he wants something, people rush to fetch it.

Now, although we may not be rich young rulers, that mind-set is not alien to us. In a sense, we have become a spoiled people who are impatient with delays, detours, or even disciplines. We want things done for us quickly and simply. The push button has become our symbol. Why wait or work for anything? "Pay one dollar down and get it now!" "Clothes cleaned in one hour." "Cars washed—two minutes." We itch for the instantaneous—instant coffee, instant biscuits, instant cereal, instant credit, instant e-mail, instant faxes. We are impatient people, looking for easy ways, shortcuts, quick results, simple solutions, and usually we want somebody else to do it for us.

I'm thinking of the family planning their vacation, who say, "We should go to London this summer. Call our travel agent. She will make all the arrangements." Or the businessman buzzing his secretary on the intercom and saying, "Wedding anniversary coming up this weekend. Pick out something nice for my wife and have it sent out." Or the children who break their new toy and say with a ho-hum shrug of the shoulders, "It's okay; Daddy can get us another one."

In something of a similar vein, the rich young ruler may have approached Jesus that day asking for eternal life, because when Jesus shows him the cost of discipleship—the commitment demanded, the effort, the change, the risk, the personal involvement, the sacrifice that touches even the pocketbook—the young man is disappointed and he turns away, trudges away, and misses his moment because he wants a religious quick fix rather than a total life commitment.

Listen! The things that matter most in life do not come quickly, easily, or simply. Not long ago, I read about a new-car owner who called an auto manufacturer. The owner said, "Was it your company that announced that you recently put a car together from start to finish in seven minutes?" "That's right, we did it!" said the executive proudly. "We put a car together from start to finish in just seven minutes." To which the caller replied, "Well, I just want you to know, I think I have that car!"

The things that matter most take time, effort, sacrifice, discipline, and deep commitment. Too much, too soon, too easily is the perfect formula for frustration, heartache, and mediocrity. When we get too easily and reach too quickly, we tend to appreciate too lightly. To be sure, some things you can get immediately by pushing buttons, or by paying money down, or by pulling out a plastic card. But the great things, the real values, do not come that way; they have to be grown and cultivated. You can get a sports car or a flat screen TV with a quick down payment, but character, morality, integrity, maturity, spiritual strength—these you have to wait for, work for, want intensely, commit to, and cultivate and grow, slowly but surely.

Sometimes our children's choirs sing an anthem called "Little by Little," and it has this significant line in it: "Good things that are here to stay, don't get done in just one day." The rich young ruler just didn't understand that being a disciple is no simple matter, that becoming spiritually mature is not instant or easy. It is costly! But it is a greater treasure by far than anything we have ever known. Let me illustrate the point further by looking with you at three things that we really need to work at and commit ourselves to if we are to attain any measure of spiritual maturity and understanding.

First, There Is Prayer

Developing a meaningful prayer life is no simple matter. It takes time and effort and energy. It takes practice.

Not long ago, I was watching a late-night TV talk show. The host was interviewing a man whose name you would recognize immediately. He is known all over the world as one of the greatest golfers of all time. He is a world-famous sports figure. He made an interesting confession on TV that night. He said, "I have never been what you'd call a real churchgoing Christian, but I do consider myself a religious man. When I was a little kid (four years old), my mother taught me a bedtime prayer, and I still say that same prayer today. It's the only one I know."

You know, that seemed kind of sad to me because that is not what happened in other areas of his life. As he grew older and stronger, he did not continue to play golf as he did when he was "a little kid." I should say not! Through hard work, practice, effort, discipline, sacrifice, and commitment, he became one of the superstar golfers in the history of sports. He became one of the finest athletes ever to walk on the face of the earth. But at the age of fifty-two, he was still repeating the same solitary prayer he had learned as a child of four. His prayer life had never grown, never stretched, never matured. It was static. There was no development at all. There is something disheartening about that, isn't there?

But who are we to throw stones at him? Most of us are in the same boat. Speaking of boats and prayer, remember the story about the two men caught in a small rowboat in the midst of a storm? As the waves rose higher and the boat threatened to capsize, the men knew that they needed help. They decided that prayer was their only hope. So in the teeth of the gale, one of them shouted, "O God, you know that I haven't bothered you for the past fifteen years, and if you'll just get us out of this mess, I promise you I won't bother you again for another fifteen years!" Somehow that fellow had missed the point of what prayer is all about, hadn't he?

Florence Allshorn said, "There is really only one test of our prayer life. Namely, do we want God? Do we want him so much that we'll go on and on if it takes five, six, ten years to find him?" If you want to become a doctor, a lawyer, a minister, a teacher, a musician, an architect, an engineer, or an athlete, it takes determination. You have to plug away at it. It doesn't come easily or simply or overnight. Maybe the same thing is true with prayer. Maybe it takes a lot of practice.

Think Next of the Scriptures

Developing a meaningful understanding of the Scriptures is no simple matter. The truth is that while the Bible is in nearly all of our homes, not all of us are at home in the Bible. How is it with you? Do you feel at home with the Scriptures? Is the Bible a friend or a stranger to you? When crisis comes, you need a friend. In desperation, people have turned to the Bible for strength, for comfort, for the word of life, expecting instant, simple solutions—and sometimes they have come up empty because they didn't know how to find its treasures.

Edward Blair, in his book *The Bible and You,* points out that:

> The person who is looking for a way to master the Bible "in three easy lessons" will be disappointed. . . . In the first place one can never "master" the Bible; one can only be mastered by it. In the second place the Bible is so incalculably rich that the human mind cannot possibly embrace it all in a few attempts. . . . Familiarity with the Bible comes by long exposure . . . to its contents." ([Nashville: Abingdon Press, 1953], p. 52)

I know a minister who does an interesting thing. In preparing for funeral services, he takes the Bible of the deceased person and skims through it to see what has been marked or underscored or written in the margin. He says that he discovers a lot about the person from his or her Bible. Interesting, isn't it? And it raises a good question: What would your Bible say about you?

Finally, Think About the Church

Being a real, committed churchperson is no simple matter. Becoming a real, devoted churchperson is a growing, developing thing. It is not a single act or event. It is not one experience that is suddenly over and done with. It is a process, a pilgrimage, a life commitment.

The initial salvation experience, however it may come and however wonderful it may be, is only the beginning; there is much to follow. It's like a wedding. It is easy to have a beautiful wedding, but it takes a lot of work and commitment and love to make a beautiful marriage.

I am convinced that many professing Christians do not understand this. They have the simplistic idea that when they have "accepted Christ" and joined the church, that's all there is and there's nothing more. They see this initial experience as the final goal when really it is only the starting place. They think they have graduated when really they have barely enrolled. It is a wonderful thing to become "newborn," to become a "babe in Christ." But to remain a spiritual baby is tragic. Babies are sweet and adorable, but if they remain infants and never grow up, we consider that a calamity, and it is.

Ernest Hemingway, the superb storyteller, won the Nobel Prize in Literature in 1954. His novel *The Old Man and the Sea* was cited. It's the story of an old man, a Cuban fisherman, who for eighty-four days had gone without a catch. On the eighty-fifth day, he went a bit farther and caught a giant marlin. It was a great struggle to land the prize catch. It took three days, but finally the old man, with his hands torn and bleeding, his body aching with pain, won the battle. He had caught the fish. He couldn't get the huge fish into his boat, so he lashed the eighteen-foot marlin to his boat and headed for home, thrilled with his victory.

But then the sharks came and feasted on his catch. When the old fisherman landed in his harbor, all that was left of his magnificent catch was a skeleton. His great earlier victory ended in dismal defeat. This story became almost an autobiography of Hemingway himself, who, seven years after his Nobel Prize, committed suicide. Somehow his early success had shriveled.

When we look around, we see the heartbreaking fact that this happens to so many people in their faith experience. They end up with only a skeleton of some earlier victory. Like the rich young ruler, they come to the Master, realizing that he has the answer to life. They have a warm and brief encounter with him, but then, unable to make the rest of the journey, they turn away sorrowfully because they want a simple, easy solution.

The truth is, it's no simple matter. When it comes to real faith and a real discipleship, we need a lasting, tenacious commitment—to prayer, to the study of the Scriptures, and to the church.

Some years ago, I went to see a play on a college campus in Tennessee. The drama students were putting on a musical called *For Heaven's Sake.* One of the pieces in the play was a song called "God's Making Us Over." The song depicts a woman asking God to come into her life and turn her life around and make her over into a new person. She says she asked God to come into her life and make just a few small changes, but God went overboard. He came in asking for lots of changes, significant changes, dramatic changes. The song concluded with the line, "God's making me over, I can't be the same anymore."

The point is, God can make us over and give us a new start. God can empower us to turn our lives around, turning away from shallow, surface religion toward a deep commitment to Christ and the church.

4

From Selfish Ambition to Humble Service

"THE MEANING OF GREATNESS"

Read Matthew 20:20-28.

Some years ago, one of our former presidents of the United States found himself in an interesting dilemma. A woman who was a friend of his family kept pestering the president to appoint her husband to the post of Secretary of Commerce. Now, the woman's husband had no political experience, no training for the job, no real expertise or qualifications to bring to the position *at all*. In fact, he was a house painter! But the woman wanted her husband to be named by the president to this key cabinet position, the Secretary of Commerce.

Now, of course, the president knew that he could not do that. He could not accommodate the woman's request. That was obvious. So, the president (kind man that he was) tried to cushion his refusal by explaining to the woman that such an important post required a person who had been prepared by long training to meet the demands of that significant job. It required, he said, a big person. This explanation didn't faze the woman one bit. That would take care of itself, she said. If the president would just appoint her husband to the position, then he would be a big person!

Now, that human interest story from American history reminds me of this story in Matthew 20, where the mother of James and John comes to Jesus and makes the request that her two sons will get the top two spots in Jesus' kingdom.

Remember the story with me. Jesus is heading toward the cross. He has "set his face toward Jerusalem." He is surely thinking deep thoughts about the dramatic showdown he will face in the Holy City in just a few days, events that will lead to his being nailed to a cross. Jesus has indicated to his disciples what lies ahead, but they don't get it. They just can't see it. They are still thinking about a powerful, luxurious military kingdom.

So, here they come, James and John and their mother, with this ambitious, presumptuous request. The mother makes the request, but (don't miss this, now) James and John are right there with her. They are all in this together. What do they want? The top two spots in this new kingdom that Jesus is about to establish, the top two spots for James and John. Jesus answers: "You don't know what you are asking."

You see, Jesus knew that they weren't seeing it clearly. They were thinking about power and position and fame and political clout, while he was thinking about sacrificial love and suffering and service. They were thinking about rising to places of prestige; he was thinking about death on a cross. They were thinking about the perks of being rulers in high places; he was thinking about serving the world by being a suffering servant. So, Jesus says to them, in effect, "You are talking the talk, but the real question is, can you walk the walk?" This is where the famous hymn " 'Are Ye Able,' Said the Master" comes from. James and John answer boldly, "Lord, we are able." That's the end of the story, and they all live happily ever after, right? No. Not quite.

The other disciples get wind of how James and John are trying to slip in ahead of them, and they don't like it. The Scriptures say they began to be indignant, angry, with James and John. So, Jesus calls them all together and gives them the lesson one more time. He says, "I've said it before, and I'll say it again: In my kingdom, true greatness is not found in fortune or fame, not found in position or power or political clout. Those things are fragile and fleeting. No, true greatness is found in 'being a servant.' " That's a hard lesson to learn, isn't it?

J. Wallace Hamilton spoke about this some years ago, and here's what he said:

> We all have the drum-major instinct. We all want to be important, to surpass others, to achieve distinction, to lead the parade. Or—as Carl Sandburg once put it—"We all want to play Hamlet." Alfred Adler, one of the fathers of modern psychiatry, names it the *dominant* impulse in human nature; he thinks the desire for recognition, the wish to be significant, is stronger than that of sex, which Freud put first. And while we may be provoked with James and John for asking Jesus to put them first—like soldiers holding up the battle until they have made sure of their promotion—we should in fairness admit that in a thousand subtle ways, we too have tried to be drum-major. (*Ride the Wild Horses* [Westwood, N.J.: Revell, 1952], p. 26)

You see, ambition, in and of itself, is a good thing, a natural, normal part of our makeup. We all want to be important. We all want to be significant. We all want to do our best. Ambition is basically a good quality. It only becomes bad when distorted or misused. When ambition becomes selfish or ruthless or cruel, then it becomes a monstrous, destructive tyrant.

That's what was brewing in the group of disciples that day. James and John (with the help of their mother) were saying, in effect, "We're going to get ahead no matter who we have to step on or push aside. If we have to elbow other people out of the way, then so be it!" There it is, the picture of ruthless, selfish ambition—and it is not a very pretty picture, is it?

But then Jesus straightens them out. He says, it's okay to be ambitious, but don't be ambitious to promote yourself. Rather, be ambitious to help others. Be ambitious to serve other people. *Selfish* ambition is blind and fraught with problems and difficulties. Now, let's break this down a bit and bring it closer to home with three thoughts.

First of All, Blind, Selfish Ambition Makes You Arrogant

Jesus once told a parable about two men who went up to the Temple to pray. One was a Pharisee, a religious leader, who prayed loudly, pompously, arrogantly. The other man was a publican, a tax collector, who prayed humbly, penitently, contritely. The parable ends by telling us that it was the humble tax collector who went home justified, rather than the arrogant Pharisee (Luke 18:9-14).

Recently, I ran across a contemporary "take-off" on this parable. It goes like this. Two men went to church to pray. One was a man named Hornblower. The other was a teacher. The man named Hornblower stood and looked heavenward, saying, "God, I thank you that I am so much better than other people. I thank you, O Lord, that I am not like the rest of humankind. And especially, I thank you that I am not like this poor teacher here who feeds off the public payroll. It's my money that pays this teacher's salary. It's my money that keeps his school and this community going. So, I thank you, Lord, that I am the great man I am and not like this poor, pitiful school man here." Hearing this, the schoolteacher humbly bowed his head and said, "Lord, have mercy, for I was that man's teacher!"

When James and John arrived that day hiding behind their mother's skirt and making this arrogant request, thinking that a person's greatness was tied to his earthly position, don't you imagine that Jesus felt like saying, "Mercy me! Haven't they been listening? Haven't they heard all of my lessons about humility and service and sacrificial love? Did they not hear me when I talked about kindness and thoughtfulness and generosity toward others? Don't they understand by now that being a "big person" does not come from holding some big position but from having a big heart? Don't they get it? Don't they see that true greatness does not come from serving yourself but from serving God and serving others?"

William Barclay put it like this:

> The world may assess a man's greatness by the number of people whom he controls and who are at his beck and call; or by his intellectual standing and his academic eminence; or by the number of committees of which he is a member; or by the size of his bank balance and the material possessions which he has amassed; but in the assessment of Jesus Christ these things are irrelevant. His assessment is quite simply—how many people have you helped?

An unknown poet expressed it like this:

> You cannot pray the Lord's Prayer
> And even once say "I."
> You cannot pray the Lord's Prayer
> And even once say "My."
> Nor can you pray the Lord's Prayer
> And not pray for another,
> For when you pray for daily bread
> You must include your brother.
> For others are included
> In each and every plea;
> From beginning to the end of it,
> It does not once say "me."

Notice that in Matthew 20:20-28 Jesus does not abolish or condemn ambition; he redeems it. Jesus says, in effect, "Be ambitious, but be ambitious for others. Be ambitious to be a servant."

Recently, I saw a family I know well. The mother was pushing her children in one of those double strollers. The little girl was five, and the little boy was two. I knelt down and said to the little girl, "My, you look so beautiful today!" and she said, "Thank you, but did you notice my little brother? He looks good, too!"

Now, that's what Jesus is after—the spirit of being ambitious to help others. Deep down, the disciples knew that. They knew that selfishness and arrogance did not really fit into his kingdom, and that's why when it was exposed, they were embarrassed. That's thought number one: Blind, selfish ambition makes you arrogant.

Second, Blind, Selfish Ambition Makes You Adversarial

Blind, selfish ambition causes you to see everyone else as the adversary, as the enemy, as the competitor. Up to this point, Peter, James, and John had been very close friends, partners, buddies, and colleagues. They were the inner circle—Jesus' closest confidants, his executive committee. But now, as they approached Jerusalem and what they thought would be the establishment of a powerful and prosperous kingdom, now, in the crucial moment when they thought the prize appointments would soon be handed out, now, in crunch time, suddenly James and John saw Simon Peter differently. Blinded by their selfish ambition, they now saw Simon Peter as the adversary, the enemy, the opponent, and they tried to elbow in ahead of him.

That's the way Mark's Gospel records it. In Mark's version of the story, it is James and John who come to Jesus with their request for the most prestigious positions (Mark

10:35-45). Matthew was so embarrassed by the blind ambition of James and John that later, when he tells the story in his Gospel (written after the Gospel of Mark), he changes it; he softens it by having the mother of James and John make the request. Matthew thought that seemed more natural, easier to swallow, because we know how moms are about their boys! But you can't really cover it. James and John were great men, great disciples to whom we owe much, but in that moment, their ambition blinded them.

Do you know Oscar Wilde's famous story that depicts the devil crossing the Libyan desert? The devil comes upon a group of people who are tormenting a holy man. They are trying to tempt him and break his spirit, but to no avail. They can't touch him. They can't upset him. They can't ruffle him. He resists every temptation with a great spirit of peace, poise, and serenity. They tempt him with all sorts of worldly pleasures, but the holy man is steadfast, unbending in his commitment.

Finally, after watching the tempters for a while, the devil whispers to them, "Your methods are too crude, too obvious. Permit me one moment." Then the devil walks over and whispers to the holy man, "Have you heard the news? Your brother has just been made Bishop of Alexandria!" Immediately, a malignant scowl of jealousy clouds the formerly serene face of the holy man (Gordon MacDonald, *The Life God Blesses* [Nashville: Thomas Nelson, 1994], p. 143). Don't miss this: Blind, selfish ambition makes you arrogant, and it makes you adversarial.

Third and Finally, Blind, Selfish Ambition Makes You Apathetic Toward Other People

There is an old story about a young man from West Virginia who went off to college at a prestigious eastern university. The mountain youngster was able to go to this highly regarded Ivy League school only because his father had been so proud of the son's academic record that he had worked many, many hours of overtime in the lumber mill in their hometown to pay for the boy's college. There were tuition and books and room and board to be paid, and the young man told his dad that you weren't anybody unless you pledged the most elite fraternity on campus. And they wanted him, and so he really needed more money—*lots* more money. And, of course, he would have to have a whole new wardrobe. The father, who had never set foot on a college campus, was excited to hear about his son's college exploits, and he said to his son, no problem, go for it. He would come up with the money. And he did, so it all worked out fine.

The young man was so caught up in his new friends that he just couldn't make it home for Thanksgiving or Christmas, but of course, he would need some more money. And then when spring break came, he called his dad and said it was most important for him to go to the beach. Everybody was going, and he would need some more money, so please, send the money quickly.

But while he was on the beach in Florida, the young man received an urgent message that his father had had a serious heart attack. He hurried home, but it was too late; his dad was gone. A few of his father's lifelong friends from the lumber mill were gathered in the hospital's waiting room. When the young man walked in, his father's best friend, Wilbur, hugged him, and as he and the other friends left the room later, Wilbur handed the young man a pile of neatly folded clothes and a pair of shoes—his father's work overalls and work boots.

As the young man sat there in the waiting room, holding his father's clothes, he noticed the boots. The boots each had a huge hole in the bottom. His father had worked each day in boots with holes in them. His father, who always seemed able to come up with the money to buy his son's khaki slacks, crisp oxford shirts, and penny loafers—that man's feet had burned from the heat of the lumber mill floor while he labored for his hourly wage to provide for his son, who just took it all for granted. And the pain was too much. The boy cried at the magnitude of his father's sacrificial love, and he cried in shame at his own apathy and preoccupation, his own selfishness and lack of appreciation. It would be a long time before he could think of his father without weeping.

I have a feeling that that's the way James and John must have felt a few days after their presumptuous request. Whey they saw the nailprints in Jesus' hands and the hole in his side, the symbols of his sacrificial love, I can just see them weeping and saying, "What were we thinking? How foolish we were! How blind!"

The point is clear: Selfish ambition can blind the best of us. It can make us arrogant, adversarial, and apathetic toward others. Now, James and John eventually saw the light. The question is, have we?

The good news is in what happened later. James and John finally "got it"; eventually they understood and embraced the message of "being ambitious to help others." They were converted from selfish ambition to humble service. They both gave their lives to Christ and his church. The "take-home value" here for you and me is simply this: God allows us to turn our lives around! God empowers us to turn our lives around! God can turn us, too, away from blind ambition and point us in the direction of sacrificial love.

5

From Self-centeredness to Christ-centeredness

"Lord, Help Me to Live for Others, That I May Live Like Thee"

Read John 13:34-35.

Last year on Mother's Day, we had some children come to the lectern in the morning worship services to talk about their love for their mothers. We did this as a complete surprise to the moms, and some of them almost fainted, but the children all did great. They gave beautiful and touching tributes to their mothers.

One said, "My mom is awesome. She rocks!"

Another said, "My mom always helps me, especially when I'm hurt."

Still another said, "I love my mom. She plays basketball with me even though she doesn't know the rules."

Then a little ten-year-old boy named Drew McKay stepped up to the lectern and said something I will never forget. He said, "I know what love is because my mother is Julie McKay." When he said that, you could have heard a pin drop in the sanctuary. That powerful comment touched my heart, and it made me think of a person who has been a close friend of our family for many years.

I thought of Mary Edna Brossette and all the things our family knows because Mary Edna was our friend. Mary Edna was a member of our church when we were in Shreveport. We first met her in 1972 when I joined the staff of that church. Immediately, Mary Edna and her husband, Marvin, welcomed us into their home and into their hearts. Over all those years, Mary Edna befriended us in amazing ways. She helped us, fed us, loved us, encouraged us. She sent us fudge and brownies and chocolate chip cookies and lemon squares and "hobo" bread—and lots of all of it.

When our granddaughter, Sarah, was born, Mary Edna was there. She was the first person outside the family to babysit Sarah, and from the very first moment, she became like a third grandmother to Sarah and, later, to all of our grandchildren.

From Mary Edna, we learned what love is, what generosity is, what hospitality is. We learned from her what it means to be a Christian friend. Mary Edna never waited around to be asked for help. She always took the initiative. She saw the need and quickly stepped up to the plate to do what needed to be done.

Sometimes a single episode in a person's life can speak volumes about the spirit of that person. In Mary Edna's life, there are so many to choose from. Let me just share two examples.

The first episode occurred when our family moved to Texas some years ago. Mary Edna and Marvin came down to Houston for a weekend. They knew we had come to a great place, but they had to come and see it with their own eyes. They came to worship with us at St. Luke's. They found June, Jodi, and Jeff and sat down front with them, and they loved it. When church was over, they went down to the Fellowship Hall for the after-church fellowship— punch, coffee, cookies, and conversation.

I got there late, and when I walked in I couldn't believe my eyes at first. The hall was jam-packed with people, and Mary Edna was at the refreshment table serving the punch. But then I thought, *Well, that's Mary Edna!* Our lay volunteer had become ill and had to leave, and Mary Edna just took over. She saw a need and she jumped into action, just like she had always done. Her first time in our church, and she gracefully and joyfully and enthusiastically went to work.

Some people go to church and say, "No one spoke to me." Mary Edna never had that problem. She took the lead, and she led with her heart. She didn't wait for someone to speak to her. She took the initiative and reached out in love and service to everyone around her. She showed in her words, her deeds, her attitudes, and her acts of loving service what it means to be a disciple of Christ.

The other episode so representative of Mary Edna's spirit occurred just before our son Jeff got married. Our granddaughter, Sarah, was two years old at the time, and two days before the wedding, Mary Edna called us. She said, "Marvin and I are coming down to the wedding a day early. We are going to take care of Sarah while you all go to the rehearsal and the rehearsal dinner. We love Sarah, and she feels comfortable with us, so you all can go and relax and have fun, and we will have fun with Sarah."

"But, Mary Edna," we said, "we heard that Marvin is in the hospital."

"He is," she said, "but he gets out in the morning, and we will just drive right down [which, by the way, was a five-hour drive]. We'll be there," she said, "You can count on us."

Sure enough, the afternoon of the rehearsal, they came driving in to meet us at the hotel where we were staying. They got out of the car, and here they came across the hotel parking lot. Marvin was still hooked up to an IV. They had it on one of those tall poles with wheels, but here they came, pushing that pole, smiling, waving, and anxious to help—and help they did!

Last May, just nine months ago, Marvin and Mary Edna went on a pleasure trip to the Ozark Mountains in Arkansas. On the Friday morning before Mother's Day, they came around a sharp turn in the mountains and saw a car coming straight at them in their lane. They hit head-on. Marvin was seriously injured in the crash, but he survived. Mary Edna didn't make it. She lost her life instantly in that accident, and all of us who knew her were devastated.

At Mary Edna's memorial service the next week, the sanctuary was packed with people who had been touched by her love and kindness and thoughtfulness. In that service, Mary Edna's daughter, Amy, shared with us the Mother's Day card she had selected for her mother, a card her mother never got to see. On the outside cover was a picture of a young woman saying, "Yikes! I'm becoming my mother!" Inside the card were these words: "I should be so lucky!"

Where did Mary Edna learn to love others the way she did? You know, don't you? She learned that at church. She learned it in Sunday school. She learned it at home. But most of all, she learned it from Jesus. She learned it from Jesus' words in John 13:34-35. Jesus was in the upper room with his disciples the evening before he went to the cross. He was giving them their final instructions and he said this: "A new commandment I give to you, that you love one another as I have loved you. By this love, all will know that you are my disciples" (John 13:34-35, paraphrased).

In the old *Cokesbury Worship Hymnal,* there is a poignant prayer-hymn that describes pretty well what Jesus is talking about here, and it describes pretty well what it means to be a Christian disciple. It's called "Others," and it has these words:

Lord, help me live from day to day
In such a self-forgetful way
That even when I kneel to pray
My prayer shall be for—Others.

Others, Lord, yes, others,
Let this my motto be,
Help me to live for others,
That I may live like Thee.

This is our calling as Christian disciples. This is the way Christ wants us to live, and he was right. It's a beautiful way to spend our days on this earth. Let me show you what I mean with three thoughts.

First of All, Loving Others Gives Joy to Life

All of our lives we have heard this: "It is more blessed (more joyful) to give than to receive," and over the years I have learned that this saying is incredibly true. And it is especially true and joyful when we reach out to others in the name and spirit of Jesus.

A Franciscan brother named Phillip Kelly was ministering to a large group of migrant workers from Puerto Rico who came every year to pick tomatoes and vegetables for a canning company. Many brought their families with them, and it was everyone's dream to eventually earn enough money to build a house back home in Puerto Rico.

Each December all the workers and their families would gather together in a church basement for a Christian party. At the party they would have a drawing. The winning family would receive an all-expenses-paid, glorious two-week vacation back home in Puerto Rico. To make the prize possible, each of the several hundred migrant-worker families would contribute five dollars or more. The custom was for the workers, as they arrived at the party, to deposit the money and a slip of paper with their family's name on it into the drawing box.

It so happened that one year the party was attended by the canning company foreman. The foreman's name was Walter Jansen. Walter Jansen was a good and kind man. He had worked closely with the migrant workers for twenty-five years, and he was about to retire. He very much loved these people, and over the years, he had befriended them and helped them in many ways, and they all loved him.

As the party was winding down, it came time for the drawing to see who among them would win the trip to Puerto Rico. Brother Kelly was called forward to pick the name of the lucky family from the box. They blindfolded him, and he reached into the box and pulled out a slip of paper. The name he drew out was that of the retiring foreman, Walter Jansen. The workers cheered and applauded and jumped up and down with joy. They hugged each other and danced around exuberantly when Walter's name was announced. They were deliriously happy for their beloved foreman.

During the commotion, Brother Phillip Kelly began to look through the slips of paper in the box. On each one in different handwriting was the name "Walter Jansen." Every family had put his name in for the big prize instead of their own. And the point is, they were so delighted, so happy, so joyful over what they had done!

That's the way it works. Helping others, serving others, encouraging others, reaching out to others, giving to others, loving others brings joy to your life.

Second, Loving Others Gives Purpose to Life

In a "Peanuts" comic strip from some years ago, Lucy decides that her little brother Linus has to learn to live without his security blanket. She asks him, "Linus, what are you going to do when you grow up? You can't walk around with that security blanket when you are an adult." Linus answers, "I'm thinking seriously about having it made over into a sport coat!" This answer does not satisfy Lucy, so while Linus is taking his nap, she steals away his blanket, takes it outside, and buries it in the ground. When Linus wakes up, he misses his blanket immediately. He goes into a claustrophobic panic. He screams, he shouts, he pounds the floor, he gasps for air, and cries, "I can't live without that blanket!" And then he faints.

Snoopy, the trusty dog, sees Linus's dilemma and rises to the occasion. He goes outside, sniffs out the blanket, digs it up, and brings it back to Linus. Linus is relieved and ecstatic. With one hand he grabs the blanket, and with the other he grabs Snoopy. He kisses Snoopy, hugs him, pats him, and he thanks him over and over and over. The last picture in the cartoon shows Snoopy lying on his back on his doghouse and thinking this thought: *Every now and then I feel that my existence is justified.*

Helping others, comforting others, giving to others, encouraging others, reaching out to others—this is indeed the justification for our existence. This is what God meant for us to do. This is what Jesus taught us to do, and that's why loving others gives joy to life and purpose to life.

Third and Finally, Loving Others Gives the Spirit of Christ to Life

Did you notice in the text from John 13 that Jesus did not just say, "Love one another"? No, he said to love one another "as I have loved you."

We are called not just to love but to *Christlike* love, and that means our love for others should be generous and gracious and compassionate and sacrificial and unconditional.

That's the way Christ loved us, and that's the way he wants us to love each other.

Earlier, I quoted that prayer-hymn called "Others." The last two lines of that hymn say it all: "Lord, . . . Help me to live for others/ That I may live like Thee." What this all means is this: As Christians, we know what love is because Jesus is our Christ. We know what love is because Jesus is our Lord and Savior.

6

From Emptiness to Zestful Living

"A Prescription for Meaningful Life"

Read Galatians 6:14-18.

Some time ago, our son Jeff called us from the hospital emergency room in Dallas. Jeff and his wife, Claire, had rushed there with their then three-year-old son, Dawson. (Let me hurry to tell you that Dawson is okay, and as Jeff said, with two active little boys this probably would not be their last trip to the emergency room.)

Dawson, as three-year-old little boys will do, had gotten hurt at home. He was playing "ghost" in his room. He had put a sheet over his head, tripped on the sheet, fell, and hit his head on the corner of a table. He had to have five stitches in the center of his forehead. As they waited for the doctor in the emergency waiting room, Dawson was not happy. His head hurt and he knew the doctor was going to work on him soon and that could be unpleasant, but then suddenly he brightened and smiled and said, "Mom and Dad, guess what? I'm going to have a Harry Potter scar!"

That evening as our daughter, Jodi, was telling her children, Sarah and Paul, what had happened to their cousin

Dawson, six-year-old Paul began to cry. Jodi picked him up
and held him and said, "Don't worry, Paul; Dawson is going
to be all right. They fixed his head at the hospital, and he
is going to be just fine." And Paul said, "That's not why I'm
crying." Confused, Jodi asked, "Well, what's the matter?
Why are you crying?" Paul said, "I'm crying because
Dawson's going to have a Harry Potter scar, and I won't
have one!"

Well, not many of us get to have a Harry Potter scar in
the center of our foreheads, but according to the Bible we
can have something much better. We can have the marks
of Jesus Christ.

The apostle Paul talked about this in his letter to the
Galatians. In essence, he said this: "Nobody has to wonder
who I am. Nobody has to ask what I stand for. Nobody
needs to question my commitment to Christ and his
church, because I have the marks of Jesus branded on my
body. Clearly I am a slave for Christ!"

In biblical times, slavery was quite common. Slaves were
regarded as pieces of property. They were marked with visible signs that dramatically indicated to whom they
belonged, who their owner was, who their master was.
Historians tell us that some slaves were marked by a brand
on the forehead, some by a tattoo on the wrist, and as
strange as it may sound to us today, another mark of slavery was a pierced ear.

Now let me hurry to say that in our world today, slavery
is not to be condoned in any way, form, or practice. But in
the time of the early church, slavery and the markings of
slavery were common, familiar, and accepted practices. It is
interesting to note that back then some of the slaves were
voluntary slaves—that is, they chose that way of life as
something of a vocation.

It is out of this background that Paul was speaking in the
sixth chapter of Galatians when he said, "Henceforth let no

[one] trouble me [or question me]; for I bear on my body the marks of Jesus" (v. 17 RSV). The Galatians had doubted Paul. They wondered about this one who had persecuted the Christians so arduously only a short time before. They questioned his theology, his apostleship, his authority. In answer, Paul said to the Galatians, "Look here! Anyone can see that I belong to Christ! Christ is my owner, my master. Christ is the Lord of my life. I am his property, I am his servant. I am the complete and devoted slave of Christ. He has claimed me, branded me, bought me with a price." Paul was saying, "As surely as you can look at a group of slaves and tell by their markings to whom they belong, even so, you can look at me and see by my markings, my visible evidence, that I am a slave of Christ. I bear on my body the marks of Jesus."

When Paul spoke of the marks of Jesus on his body, he was probably referring to the physical scars he had received because of his consecration to Christ. Physical scars from beatings, floggings, shipwrecks, harsh persecution, all prompted by his unflinching allegiance to Jesus Christ. But also remember that when Paul used the word "body," he doesn't just mean flesh and blood. He meant total personality, all that we are and all that we have and all that we will ever become.

So when Paul said, "I bear on my body the marks of Jesus," he meant that Christ had claimed his heart, his mind, his soul, his strength, his attitudes, his abilities, his whole being, his total personality. He meant that the spirit of Christ had pervaded every aspect of his life, that in all he was and did, he was the complete slave of Christ.

Now, let me ask you something. Be honest now: How is it with you? Can people look at you today and tell by visible evidence that you are a Christian? Can people tell by the way you act, by the way you speak, by the way you live and relate to others that you are the servant of Christ? Do you in your total personality bear the marks of Christ? Well, what are they? What are the present-day marks of Christ?

There are many, but for now let me list three that together serve as a neat, easy-to-remember prescriptions for meaningful life: a self we can live with, a faith we can live by, a love we can live out. These are dramatic marks of Christlike living.

First, a Self We Can Live With

"A self we can live with" means to live in the Christlike spirit of integrity, honesty, and high moral character. It is a distinguishing mark of Christlike living because as we study the Gospels, we see clearly that Jesus lived daily on the highest level of personal righteousness.

Last Tuesday morning, I was driving back from a meeting in East Texas. I was listening to a Dallas–Fort Worth radio station, and I heard a poignant news story about some math students at Dunbar High School in Fort Worth. Dunbar High School is noted for its great basketball program, but this story was about a team of math students the school had sent to participate in the University Interscholastic League State Calculator Championship.

In this competition, high-school students sit down in front of their calculators, and in just thirty minutes, they answer eighty questions in algebra, geometry, and physics. One of the Dunbar students registered the highest individual score, and at the end of the round, the Dunbar team was in first place by one point. They declared a break, after which the Dunbar team would be presented their first-place gold medals as State Champions. However, during the intermission, one of the Dunbar students realized that a mistake had been made by the judges and that, on the official score sheet, their team had accidentally been given two extra points that they were not supposed to receive. (How ironic that the judges at a math competition made a mathematical error!)

But what should the student do? If he didn't say anything, who would know? Nobody would ever notice, and his team would win the gold medal. On the other hand, if he reported the error, his team would lose the two points and drop to second place.

He conferred with his teammates, and they decided that the honest and honorable thing to do was to tell the judges the truth. With their coach, they reported the mistake. They said the competition director looked at them strangely, but they also said, "We knew it was the right thing to do, and we are glad we did it."

At the awards ceremony, first place and the gold medals went to another high school, from Longview, and the Dunbar team came in second. The young high-school student who had seen the mistake was asked why he had reported it, and he said, "It was the guilt factor. Twenty years from now," he said, "I would have looked at that gold medal and felt guilty because I would know we didn't really win. Reporting it was the right thing to do. I had to do it because I have to live with myself, and I wanted to be able to look at myself in the mirror and not feel ashamed." That's pretty mature for a seventeen-year-old high-school senior who already knows the meaning of integrity.

The poet Edgar A. Guest put it like this:

> I have to live with myself, and so
> I want to be fit for myself to know.

This is one very important mark of Christlike living. We can call it "honesty" or "character" or "integrity," or we can call it "a self we can live with."

Second, a Faith We Can Live By

This is another dramatic mark of Christlike living. Throughout his life, and especially in the crisis moments toward the end, Jesus displayed an incredible trust in the Father. This trust was what gave him that strong spirit of confidence, poise, and serenity that provided him the amazing ability to face adversity and threats and persecution, and even death, with strength, peace, and blessed assurance.

That is precisely what the Christian faith does for us. It gives us the strength and power to face every circumstance of this life, and even the circumstances beyond this life, with courage and confidence.

Two old farmers were sitting on the porch, watching the rain pelt down, and this conversation took place.

"Whatcha gonna do if the river overflows?"
"Sit on the gallery and watch it go."
"Whatcha gonna do if your hogs all drown?"
"Wish I'd lived on higher ground."
"Whatcha gonna do if your cow floats away?"
"Throw in after her a bale of hay."
"Whatcha gonna do if your cabin leaves?"
"Climb up on the roof and straddle the eaves."
"Whatcha gonna do when it come on night?"
"Trust in God and hold on tight."
"But whatcha gonna do if your strength gives 'way?"
"Say, 'Howdy, Lord, it's Judgment Day!'"

I like that old poem because it's about a faith to live by. It's about trusting God. It's about doing our best and trusting God for the rest. It's about counting on God and believing that nothing, not even death, can separate us from God and his love. We can trust God come what may, and he will always be there for us.

That attitude of trust is a key to life. It gives us a confidence that is amazing. Someone once asked a famous Christian gentleman why he was so serene and confident all the time. He said simply but profoundly, "I'm a Christian, and I trust God."

Let me ask you something: Do you bear in your life these marks of Jesus—a self you can live with and a faith you can live by?

Third and Finally, a Love We Can Live Out

Remember how the hymn writer put it: "They will know we are Christians by our love."

Some years ago when the Vietnam War was winding down, a large number of Vietnamese refugees came to America to make a new start with their lives. The church we were serving at the time adopted one of these families to help them get established in their new land. The family had two children the same ages as our children (eleven and eight). One Saturday morning, we took the children shopping in a nearby mall. The Vietnamese children had never seen an escalator before, and they were fascinated by this moving stairway. The little girl, age eleven, watched the people going up and down and asked me lots of questions.

Meanwhile, the little boy, who was eight, just kept watching the moving escalator handrail. Finally, I asked them if they were ready to move on, and the little girl said, "Yes." But the little brother just stood there and kept staring at the moving handrail. Again, I asked, "Are you ready to go now and see something else?" And he answered, "I'm waiting for my gum to come back."

Well, it did come back, but I gave him a new piece of gum. There's a sermon there, somewhere. It shows that boys and girls are different, but also it reminds us that what we send out comes back. We see it in Jesus' parable of the prodigal son (Luke 15:11-32). The father sent out love, and love came back to bless him with a big celebration. The elder brother sent out resentment, it came back to haunt him; it caused him to miss the party.

Some years ago, Albert Schweitzer was speaking to a graduating class at a prestigious college in London when he said, "Some of you will be highly successful. Some of you will make a lot of money. Some of you will rise to places of prominence. Some of you will be adorned with titles . . . but I promise you this: only those of you who learn how to serve will be happy."

It's a key to life—learning how to serve, learning how to live unselfishly, learning how to *love!* You want to have a meaningful life, a productive life, a fulfilling life, a happy life? Here's how to do it: Bear on your body these three marks of Christlike living—a self you can live with, a faith you can live by, and a love you can live out.

7

From Silly Fretting to Creative Worrying

"How to Improve Your Worrying"

Read Matthew 6:25-34.

Not too long ago I was in a meeting at the Medical Center. Doctors and other medical experts were expressing great concern about the fact that since September 11, 2001, there had been an alarming increase in requests by people for pharmaceuticals. It seems that more and more people were requesting antidepressant medicines because they were worried and depressed and scared about what the September 11 terrorist attacks had done to our world.

Now, let me hurry to say that the worry habit is not a new thing. It has been with us for quite some time. But for many people, the horrendous events of September 11 and the ongoing threat of terror have amplified the anxiety and turned up the worry-meter several notches.

Now, the quick fix, the simplistic solution is to say to these people, "Don't worry! Don't worry!" Everywhere we go these days, we are bombarded with this message, "Don't worry!" For example, go to the bookstore, and you will find all kinds of self-help books on this subject, books like *How to Stop Worrying and Start Living*; *How to Kick the Worry-Habit*; *Spiritual Vitamins for Worriers*; *How to Trust More and*

Worry Less; and, of course, this classic—*How to Cope When You're as Worried as a Long-tailed Cat in a Room Full of Rocking Chairs.*

Or go to the drugstore, and you will see all kinds of medicines designed to reduce tension, anxiety, and worry, numerous prescriptions and medical aids to calm us down, to settle our fears, to help us sleep, to ease our stress, and to relieve our apprehensions. Even bumper stickers preach about this. I saw one the other day that read "Worry is like a rocking chair—it's something to do, but it won't get you anywhere!" Another read "Stop Stewing and Start Cooking."

Now, the very fact that so much is being written or prescribed with regard to the problem of worry tells us something. It tells us that there is a big market out there for these books and medicines and bumper stickers, that there are lots of folks out there these days who feel plagued with the agony of worry, that there are large numbers of chronic worriers in our world today who are screaming for help and looking for answers. It tells us that we who live in this stressful world not only worry, but we also worry that we are *worrying* too much.

Now, hold on to your seat, because I want to tell you something that I think is tremendously important about this. You may soon forget much of what you read in this chapter, but I hope you will long remember this. Are you ready? Here it is: Even though it is said to us over and over, "Don't worry, don't worry," *the truth is that we cannot stop worrying.* We cannot stop worrying, because God has put within us (for our own good) a certain amount of worry energy or anxiety energy. We all have worry energy naturally within us. It is part of our basic makeup, and it's there for good reason. So, the question is not *will* we worry—we will! We can count on that. The question is, how do we use our worry energy creatively? How do we use our worry energy productively? The question is, *Are we directing our worry energy toward the real priorities of life?* The question is, *Are we letting our worry energy motivate us and pull us up into positive action rather than deplete us and push us down into self-pity?* The problem is not that we worry but that many of us do not know how to worry meaningfully, or how to put our worries to work, or how to use this God-given anxiety energy for good.

If we never worried about our children, we would be terrible parents. If we had no concern for our city or our nation or our world, we would be awful citizens and naïve characters. If we never worried about our jobs or had no consideration for a job well done, we would be pitiful workers. If we had absolutely no concern for our church, we would be pathetic church members. If we never worried about making ends meet, we would be in big trouble. The key is to learn how to worry creatively. Jesus gives us some great lessons about this in Matthew 6. Let me outline his message for us.

First, to Worry Creatively Means to Let Our Worries Work for Us Rather Than Against Us, to Let Our Worries Move Us to Action

Now, let me hurry to emphasize that there is a huge difference between creative worry and silly fretting. Creative worry spurs us into action. Silly fretting handcuffs us, imprisons us, and immobilizes us. In the Sermon on the Mount in Matthew 6:25, when Jesus says, "Do not be anxious" (RSV), he is not talking about creative worry. He is not talking about thoughtful consideration or loving concern or careful, sensible planning. Rather, he is talking about silly, useless, immature fretting. The Greek word used here for "anxious" is a fascinating and revealing one. It is *merimnao*, a combination of two shorter Greek words—

merige, which means "to divide," and *nous*, which means "the mind." In other words, Jesus is saying, "Beware the divided mind. Don't get your priorities mixed up." Someone expressed it in a poem called "The Worry Cow," which goes like this:

The worry cow would have lived 'til now
If she hadn't lost her breath.
But she thought her hay wouldn't last all day,
So she mooed herself to death.

That kind of worry can kill. It robs us of our vitality and poise and the ability to think straight. It makes emotional wrecks of us, takes away the radiance of living, and makes us mere skeletons of our real selves.

The noted writer Thomas Carlyle once built a sound-proof room in his home in London so he could do his work without interference from outside noises. The reason he did this was because his neighbor had a rooster, and the rooster's crowing bothered Carlyle. Carlyle protested to the neighbor, but the neighbor answered that his rooster crowed only three times a day, and surely that was not a great annoyance. "But," Carlyle said to him, "If you only knew what I suffer just waiting for that rooster to crow!"

Many of us can relate to that, can't we? We wait and worry, just knowing that something terrible is going to happen to us at any moment. We wait and wait and worry and worry, and thus our energies are washed out and our strength depleted. But take a close look at the things that fret you. Do they really happen?

An old newspaper used to carry these words at the top of its front page: "I am an old man. I have worried a great deal about many things, most of which never happened." Ian McLaren wrote: "What does your anxiety do? It does not empty tomorrow of its sorrow; but, oh, it empties today of

64

its strength. It does not make you escape the evil, it makes you unfit to cope with it when it comes." This kind of silly, useless, immature fretting is what Jesus is warning us about here in Matthew 6 when he says, "Do not be anxious."

But, there is another kind of concern, another kind of worry that is actually productive, the worry that spurs us to action, the concern that motivates us to do something creative and productive. For example, if I never worried, I would never write a sermon. To get it done, to get it completed, to get it right, I have to get anxious about it. That worry energy, that anxiety energy, that concern prompts me, stirs me, moves me to get with the program and to get done what needs to be done.

That old Nike™ television commercial makes the point. It encouraged us to get in shape, and the theme was, "Just do it!" That's the bottom line—just do it. The point is, we can stew and fret about needing to exercise more, or we can just do it.

So first, creative worry means to let our worries work for us rather than against us, to let our worries move us to action. Now, here is the second lesson.

Second, Creative Worry Means to Let Our Worries Be Directed Toward Matters That Really Matter

Let me ask you something. What are you worried about right now? A dent in the car? A health problem? The world situation? The economy? Your vacation? The weather? Your next hair appointment? A party invitation? A problem at work? The homeless? The hungry? The kingdom of God? Your marriage? Your children? Your favorite sports team? Where to have lunch? Or how long this chapter is? You see, our worry list says a lot about us and about our priorities. What we are anxious about right now reveals a lot about what is really important to us.

Jesus preached his greatest sermon to the world's great worriers. The people who heard him that day when he preached the Sermon on the Mount were people who worried themselves silly over countless washings, keeping minute laws, fasts, feasts, and traditions. And they were fretful over social status and taxes and money and death. Really, their list of worries was not so different from ours. And Jesus said to them and to us: "Don't be so anxious. Don't be so nervous. Don't be so fretful!"

He also gave us a magnificent solution. He said, "Seek first God's kingdom and his righteousness and everything else will fall into place for you. Just make God the King of your life; work at that, set your mind on that, and God will bring it out right. Do the best you can each day and then turn it over to God" (Matthew 6:33, paraphrased).

I remember as a child going to the circus where they would have these chameleons that could change their colors to match their environment. Put them on a brown coat and they would turn brown. Put them on a green coat and they would turn green. Well, Carl Sandburg once told of a chameleon that made it just fine changing his colors to match his environment until one day he accidentally crawled onto a plaid sport coat. The chameleon had a nervous breakdown heroically trying to relate to everything at once! Some of our worries are simply the consequence of forgetting our priorities.

To worry creatively means, first, to let our worries work for us rather than against us and, second, to let our worries be directed toward matters that really matter.

Third and Finally, Creative Worry Means to Let Our Worries Bring Us Back to God

Abraham Lincoln expressed it like this: "I have been driven many times to my knees by the overwhelming conviction that I had nowhere else to go."

Some years ago a young man named George Matheson entered Glasgow University. He had a keen mind. His hopes were high. Soon he and his fiancée would be married. He dreamed of a bright future. But then misfortune came his way. He began losing his sight, and then, it is popularly believed, when his fiancée learned of his impending blindness, she said she couldn't marry a blind man, and she left him.

Matheson's world crumbled at his feet. Devastated, afraid, and worried, he turned to God as never before, and God was there. Hurt, rejected, and without sight, George Matheson reached out in the darkness and found that God's love is always there for us, and later he would write what has become one of our most beloved hymns, a hymn sung by Christians everywhere, that says it all, a hymn of praise to God:

O Love that wilt not let me go,
I rest my weary soul in thee;
I give thee back the life I owe,
that in thine ocean depths its flow may richer, fuller be.
("O Love That Wilt Not Let Me Go")

That is the answer to the problem of worry, the "blessed assurance" that no matter what difficulties we have to face, God will always be there for us, God will always see us through. We can claim that promise, and we can live in that confidence.

So, let your worry energy move you to action, move you to the real priorities of life, and move you back home to God.

8

From the Good Fridays of the World to the Easter Sundays of the World

"WE TOO CAN BE RESURRECTED!"

Read Mark 16:1-8.

Do you remember the legend of the touchstone? It's a great story to recall—especially at Easter—but really, at any time. According to that ancient legend, if you could find the touchstone on the coast of the Black Sea and hold it in your hand, everything you touched would turn to gold. You could recognize the touchstone by its warmth. The other stones would feel cold, but when you picked up the touchstone, it would turn warm in your hand.

Once a man sold everything he had and went to the coast of the Black Sea in search of the touchstone. He began immediately to walk along the shoreline, picking up one stone after another in his diligent and intentional search for the touchstone. He was consumed with this dream. He wanted desperately to find this miraculous stone. However, after several days had passed, he suddenly realized that he was picking up the same stones again and again. So he devised a plan: He would pick up a stone, and if it was cold, he would throw it into the sea. This he did for weeks and weeks.

Then one morning he went out to continue his search for the touchstone. He picked up a stone; it was cold, and he threw it into the sea. He picked up another stone; cold. He threw it into the sea. He picked up another stone; it turned warm in his hand, and before he realized what he was doing, he threw it into the sea!

That's a good parable for us because that can so easily happen to us. We can come upon a miraculous moment like Easter, we can feel it turn warm in our hands, but then (so dulled by the routine) before we realize what we are doing, we throw it away. Absentmindedly, mechanically, nonchalantly, we toss it aside and miss the miracle.

Please don't let that happen to you. Don't miss it. Don't throw it away. As never before, no matter what month or day of the year, seize and celebrate and embrace the incredible good news of Easter. Here we find one of the greatest nuggets of God's truth—namely, that God has the power to redeem. God can, through the miracle of grace, turn bad things into good things. God can change things and make things better for you.

On Easter morning, the women came to the tomb in sadness, in defeat, in grief, in disillusionment. But there they found out firsthand about God's power to redeem. There at the empty tomb on Easter morning, they found out dramatically that God can turn defeats into victories, despair into hope, and death into life. God has the power to redeem. God can turn the heartache of Good Friday into the "Hallelujah" chorus of Easter morning.

In 1986, the third baseman for the San Francisco Giants, Bob Brenly, set a Major League record with four errors in one game at third base, against the Atlanta Braves. But then at his last time at bat, in the bottom of the ninth inning, the count was three and two; Bob Brenly hit a home run and won the game 7 to 6; from goat to hero with one swing of the bat! As Bob Brenly circled the bases with his game-winning home run, the radio announcer said, "Well, folks, Bob Brenley just redeemed himself." A bad day turned around. The jeers turned to cheers. A nightmare became the dream of a lifetime.

Now, in sports, a player may be able to redeem himself and turn it around by his own ability, but when it comes to our souls, when it comes to our spiritual lives, only God can redeem. Only God can save. Only God can turn defeat into victory, death into life. This is the message of Holy Week: "For God so loved the world that he gave his only Son, that whoever believes in him should not perish but have eternal life" (John 3:16 RSV). This is the message of Easter: " 'O death, where is thy victory? O death, where is thy sting?' . . . Thanks be to God, who gives us the victory through our Lord Jesus Christ" (1 Corinthians 15:55, 57 RSV). "Do not be alarmed; you are looking for Jesus. . . . He has been raised; he is not here'" (Mark 16:6). "Why do you look for the living among the dead? He is not here, but has risen" (Luke 24:5). He lives, and because he lives, we too can live through faith in him. We too can be resurrected.

God has the power to redeem. That's the good news of our faith, isn't it? It means that no defeat needs to be final, no heartache has to last forever. Good Fridays will come into our lives, but if we hang in and trust God, he has an Easter morning waiting for us on the other side. Through the miracle of God's grace, we can bounce back, we can change, we can start over, we can have a new beginning, a new life, we can turn around.

When you stop to think about it, God's redemptive power is absolutely amazing. And once each year, along comes Easter to remind us of that. Let me show you what I mean.

First of All, Easter Reminds Us
That Events Can Be Redeemed

We see this graphically in the painful events of Holy Week: treachery, deceit, jealousy, betrayal, denial, lies, bribed witnesses, trumped-up charges, false accusations, and a fixed trial led to the crucifixion of one who was totally innocent. Terrible events. But God somehow redeemed those events and miraculously brought good out of them. God has the power to do that. Let me show you what I mean.

Rosemary Brown is one of our finest ministers today. She serves a church in Tennessee and has been a featured speaker recently on the national radio broadcast "The Protestant Hour." Rosemary Brown tells a story about an event that happened when she was eight years old, an event that touched her life and changed her life forever.

There was a little boy who lived in her neighborhood. His name was Jeter. Jeter was an only child of well-to-do parents who made sure he received everything his little heart desired. Well, one day his little heart desired the very thing that eight-year-old Rosemary Brown's heart desired. It was a drum that had suddenly appeared in the display window at Penney's department store. It was white with blue stars and had a red, white, and blue strap that went around your neck to hold the drum in place. There were two drumsticks for beating out the rhythm, and Rosemary Brown was certain that she would lead the parade if she just owned this drum. Oh my, Rosemary wanted that drum so much she could taste it!

At dinner that night, Rosemary told her father about the drum and how much she wanted it. Her father asked how much it cost. When Rosemary told him it would cost twenty dollars, her father said in a kind of sad voice, "We'll see, honey, we'll see."

Then the very next day, Rosemary heard a sound out in the front yard, a loud noise. She looked out, and can you believe it? There stood Jeter with her drum around his neck. Jeter was beating out a *rat-a-tat-tat* and shouting for all the kids in the neighborhood to come and join his parade. Rosemary's heart was absolutely broken, and she made up her mind to put Jeter in his place once and for all.

So she gathered up all her playmates on C Street, and she devised a plan. She told the other kids that they would all fall in line behind Jeter but, when they got in front of Mrs. Hilt's house, they would all duck behind the privet hedge in her yard and leave spoiled Jeter out in the street marching by himself.

Well, Jeter started strutting down the street, his head thrown back and his knees flying up as he beat out that *rat-a-tat-tat* on his new drum. Rosemary and her friends all followed in line, marching behind Jeter, excited about their plan to desert him. When they got to the privet hedge, Rosemary gave her prearranged signal, and one by one, all of the children left the parade and hid, trying hard not to giggle out loud. They were so proud because their trick was working perfectly.

Jeter just kept on marching all alone. When Jeter reached the end of the street he looked back. He turned around and saw that he had been deserted by all of the others. Then he did something that Rosemary had not counted on. At the age of eight years old, she was not prepared for what happened next. Jeter's little arms dropped to his sides, and in a voice Rosemary would never forget, Jeter whimpered, "Little Band, where are you?" And then as if to punish Rosemary for the rest of her life, Jeter started crying.

That was a crossroads moment for Rosemary Brown. Never before in her eight years of life had she intentionally hurt another human being the way she hurt little Jeter that day. She had premeditated his downfall as the neighborhood kid who always got what he wanted, but she didn't like the way that felt. It was not fun at all. It was terrible, and she felt horrible. And that day, even though she was only eight, she made up her mind never again to intentionally hurt another person as long as she lived. She asked God to forgive her and to help her to be on the side of helping people, not hurting them.

God redeemed that event because Rosemary Brown grew up to become one of the most loving, compassionate, caring pastors in the church today. That's what Easter is about, isn't it? How God in his power and grace can take bad things and turn them into good things, how God can redeem events!

Second, Easter Reminds Us That Things Can Be Redeemed

Think of that: God can even redeem material things. For example, I'm thinking of John Wesley's study desk on display in his home in London. It's a prime example. That same desk once belonged to a bookie. Designed originally for taking gambling bets, it was redeemed to be a place of spiritual power where John Wesley thought through and wrote down his greatest sermons.

I'm thinking also of a little church in the South Pacific. They have there an unusual baptismal font. It's a large stone, deeply stained, with a portion of the top hollowed out to hold water. It was once called the Killing Rock. It was the place where cannibals brought their victims for the kill. Now it's a place where parents bring their babies to be baptized in the church.

Mostly, though, I'm thinking of the cross. The cross, once the emblem of suffering and shame and punishment and death, has been redeemed and now is the symbol of love and victory and forgiveness and life and salvation.

So you see, events can be redeemed, and things can be redeemed.

Third and Finally, People Can Be Redeemed

Easter reminds us that people like you and me can be redeemed. We don't have to stay the way we are. We can be forgiven, reshaped, reclaimed, resurrected. Be honest with yourself: Is there something in your life that needs to be changed? Is there a secret sin, a vengeful spirit, a bad temper, a lack of commitment, a hateful attitude in you that you would be a whole lot better off without? If you'll let him, God can change you. He can bring you out of the tombs that imprison you. He can empower a turnaround in your life.

Occasionally I pass through a part of our city that is anything but beautiful. It's the place where they dump scrap iron, old bottles, cans, rags, wrecked cars, and broken machinery. Recently while going by, I saw great quantities of scrap iron being loaded onto a railroad car. This scrap iron was going to a factory to be reclaimed, to be melted down and remade into something new. It may come out as surgeons' tools, or fenders for a new car, or maybe even as a steeple for a church. Who knows what it may be, but it will be new and useful and valuable.

Now, if we can do that with our old scrap iron, how much more can God do with human beings, with people like you and me! You know, he *wants* to. God wants to reclaim us. He wants to reshape us. He wants to redeem us. He is risen. He lives. He wants us to rise and live, too.

9

From Doubt to Faith

"Good News for the Doubting Thomases of the World"

Read John 20:24-29.

Over the years, I have noticed that there are two very different kinds of skeptics, as far as religion is concerned. On the one hand there are the Angry Doubters. They don't believe, and they don't care—and there is really not much you can do about them until somehow their attitude changes.

For example, recently a newspaper offered a prize for the best definition of life. Most of the responses were beautiful, but some were alarmingly negative and discouraging. For instance, one said, "Life is a bad joke that isn't even funny." Another said, "Life is a disease for which the only cure is death." Still another said, "Life is a jail sentence that we get for the crime of being born."

Now, there is not much you can do with that kind of angry, bitter, cynical skepticism. But on the other hand, there is a second group of skeptics that we might call the Honest Doubters. These are people who genuinely want to believe, but find it hard, and they wonder, they question, they brood, and they doubt. These people get close to me. My heart goes out to them. They remind me of that man in

Mark 9, who, wanting Jesus to heal his epileptic son, cries out in desperation, "I believe; help my unbelief!" (verse 24).

Also, these Honest Doubters remind me of the college sophomore who came to see me a few years ago. He said he had been to college and he didn't want to scare me but he had some questions about religion. I told him that people with questions about religion don't scare me. What scares me is the guy who thinks he has all the answers—now, *that's* the scary guy! But even more, these Honest Doubters remind me of doubting Thomas in John 20. What a fascinating character he is! *Sesame Street* has its Oscar the Grouch. Snow White and the Seven Dwarfs have their Grumpy. Charlie Brown and the "Peanuts" kids have their Lucy. And the early disciples have their doubting Thomas.

As we might expect, it is Thomas who is the last of the disciples to believe the Resurrection—and then, only after dramatic proof. When the risen Lord first appeared to his followers, one man was missing: skeptical, brooding, pessimistic doubting Thomas! Can't you see him walking gloomily through the dark streets of Jerusalem, sadly thinking back over what had happened? Can't you hear Thomas muttering, "I should have known this wouldn't work! It was all too idealistic. It was all too good to be true. And now this incredible rumor—this women's talk of resurrection. What do they know? I was there. I saw it with my own eyes. It was a ghastly sight, this crucifixion business. I saw the nails in his hands; I saw the spear in his side; I heard the Master cry out! I'll never believe again. I've seen what this world does to goodness. These are hard times, tough times. It's over now. Dead people don't rise, not when Romans kill them!"

Can't you just see Thomas moping and suffering through the darkness alone? Not wanting to face the others, brooding in solitude, tears streaming down his cheeks, wanting to be left alone, a bit like a wounded dog that crawls under the house to suffer and die out of sight.

Then, when the other disciples come to tell him that they have seen the Lord and have talked with him, Thomas just can't believe it. He wants to believe, but deep down in his cynical nature, he just can't accept it. He is sure that they have been dreaming, or hallucinating, or something. "Impossible!" he says to them. And then he blurts out those words that have stayed with him over all these years: "Unless I see the mark of the nails in his hands, and put my finger in the mark of the nails and my hand in his side, I will not believe" (John 20:25).

Doubting Thomas; he is an interesting character, isn't he? Can you identify with him? I guess we all can in varying degrees of intensity. I guess there is something of doubting Thomas in all of us. Like Thomas, we all have our moments of despair and skepticism. Doubting Thomas—the gospel has good news even for him, even for the somber pessimist.

We are going to get to that in a moment, but before we do, I want us to look first at a rather basic question, namely this: What is it that produces a doubter? Run that through your computer and see what you come out with. What produces a doubter? What causes people to be doubting Thomases?

Well, let's "go to school" on Doubting Thomas. What can we learn from his experience? Eventually, he got there. At the end of the story, he falls down before the risen Christ and makes one of the greatest affirmations in all the Bible. He says, "My Lord and my God!" (John 20:28). But why was it so hard at first for Thomas to believe? Let me list three ideas that speak to this, and I'm sure you will think of others.

First of All, Thomas Had Trouble Believing at First Because He Was a Dropout

This is indeed a big problem for many people. They drop out of the church. They quit. They run away. They detach themselves from the fellowship of believers. They pull back from their faith-support group, and as a result, malignant tentacles of doubt creep in and take over. Look at Thomas. The risen Christ came to the disciples, to the church community, that night in the upper room (see John 20:19-24). He startled them, surprised them, renewed them, resurrected them, but Thomas missed out simply because he was not there. Thomas missed it because he was absent.

What about us? How many great moments have we missed out on because we weren't there in church? Ministers love this part of the story. When we want to dramatize and underscore the importance of church attendance, the importance of the church fellowship, the significance of being involved in the church family, we like to point to Thomas and say, "Look at what Thomas missed because he had dropped out. He missed the miracle. He missed the moment. He missed the risen Christ, simply because he wasn't there, because he had dropped out of the church, because he had detached himself from the fellowship of believers."

Why do people doubt? Why do they have trouble believing? Why do they have a hard time "hanging in there"? There are many reasons, of course, but often it is simply that they have dropped out of the church. They are living in a moral fog, a state of confusion and uncertainty, because they have lost their support system.

Let me say something to you with all the feeling I have in my heart: Please don't let that happen to you. Please don't drop out. Don't lose your church. Don't cut yourself off from the roots of faith. If you are in church, please stay there. If you have somehow dropped out or slipped away, or just gotten out of the habit, please come back. Or if you have never really gotten into the church, there's no better time than now. The church wants you and will welcome you with open arms, but more than that—*God* wants you and welcomes you with open arms.

This is the first lesson we learn here. Some, like Thomas, have a hard time believing at first, and they have a hard time hanging in there because they have dropped out of the church.

Second, Thomas Had Trouble Believing at First Because He Mistakenly Assumed That the Only Truth Is Scientific Truth

The real truth is that the things we value most cannot be proved in a scientific laboratory. Scientific methods are valuable, to be sure, but they are not the only road to truth. In my opinion, the most important truths cannot be scientifically documented. The love of a woman for a man, and a man for a woman—you can't put that under a microscope, but I believe it's real.

The warmth a mother feels for her child—you can't really examine that with a magnifying glass, but I believe it's real. Honesty, courage, penitence, forgiveness, morality, love, faith, goodness, humility, grace, self-sacrifice, commitment, mercy, loyalty, compassion, kindness; these can't be put into a test tube, and yet they are the things that matter most, and they represent the greatest truths in the world.

Please don't misunderstand me. I am not knocking scientific truth or the scientific method—I am all for it. All truth is God's truth. I am simply saying that there is a special brand of truth and reality that cannot be contained in a laboratory. Remember how Jesus said it to Thomas: "'Have you believed because you have seen me? Blessed are those who have not seen and yet have come to believe'" (John 20:29).

Thomas had a hard time at first because he was a dropout and because he mistakenly assumed that the only truth is scientific truth. That brings us to a third and final thought.

Third, Thomas Had Trouble Believing at First Because He Thought Death Was the End of Life

Thomas had not experienced the good news of Easter yet, the good news that Christ has conquered death and that, through faith in him, we can have that victory too.

No other picture captured the tragedy and the heart-break of the 1995 Oklahoma City bombing than the one of the firefighter carrying that little baby girl away from the rubble of that bombed-out building. The day before the bombing, the little girl had celebrated her first birthday, the only one she would ever have on this earth. Her mother, fighting through her indescribable grief, spoke through her tears and said this: "The only way I can make it, the only thing that keeps me going, is that I know she is in heaven now with God and God will take care of her." For the Christian, death is not the end of life. It is simply moving through a door called death into a new dimension of life with God.

Some years ago, I received a letter from a good friend. His mother had died, and after her funeral someone had sent him a copy of Henry Van Dyke's "Parable of Immortality." It meant a lot to my friend, and he shared it with me. The great writer Henry Van Dyke, reflecting on the meaning of death and immortality, wrote these power-ful words:

> I am standing on the seashore. A ship at my side spreads her white sails to the morning breeze and starts for the blue ocean. She is an object of beauty and strength, and I stand and watch until at last she hangs like a speck of white cloud just where the sea and sky come down to mingle with each other. Then someone at my side says, "There she goes!" "Gone where?" Gone from my sight . . . that is all. She is just as large in mast and hull and spar as she was when she left my side and just as able to bear her load of living freight

to the place of destination. Her diminished size is in me, not in her. And just at the moment when someone at my side says, "There she goes!" there are other eyes watching her coming and other voices ready to take up the glad shout, "Here she comes!"

This is the good news of our Christian faith. When we commit our lives to Christ, God will always be there for us, even on the other side of the grave. So when life takes the wind out of our sails, we can sail on because God will send the strong breeze of his Holy Spirit to lift us and carry us and see us through.

10

From Fretfulness to Courage

"The Answer, My Friend, Is Blowin' in the Wind"

Read Acts 2:1-4.

Pat Crenshaw is her name. She is a talented musician and comedienne from Dallas. She is just a lot of fun. She always delights her audience, using funny hats and funny songs and funny stories.

I saw Pat perform at a conference a few years ago. As always, she was hilarious, and she brought down the house with her special brand of humor. At the end of her concert, she said that she would like to end her performance by giving us a "devotional thought for the day." She said that she had noticed over the years that one of our greatest temptations is to throw in the towel and quit on life. It's the temptation to give up and give in and give out, the temptation to just sit down and become a passive and bored spectator rather than an active, joyful participant. Then she said this: "God gave each of us two ends—one to think with, and one to sit on. Our success depends on which one we use the most: heads you win, tails you lose!"

In a sense, this is what the day of Pentecost is about. The disciples were spiritually bankrupt. Their minds were confused. Their confidence was shaken. Their nerves were jangled. Their strength was sapped. Their energy was depleted. Their hearts were empty, and they were tempted to just give up and sit down. Over the preceding few weeks, they had been on this unbelievable emotional roller-coaster ride, with all its incredible ups and downs. Just think of it, there was the triumphal entry into Jerusalem on Palm Sunday—that was exhilarating and glorious.

But then it was quickly followed by the arrest, the trial, and the conviction of Jesus, their Lord. They had not counted on all that. It wasn't in their game plan; it shook them; it scared the life out of them.

As if that weren't enough, next came Good Friday and the Crucifixion. That was the toughest blow of all. Their hopes were dashed, their dreams destroyed, their spirits crushed.

But then came Easter morning. Their Lord was resurrected, and their spirits were resurrected too. They were ready now to take on the world. But then came another jolt. Jesus said, "I can't stay with you. I must go to my Father, and I want you to take up this torch. I want you to take up this ministry of love. I want you to do it now. I want you to teach the world this message of love and sacrifice and commitment and grace. I want you to be my witnesses to all the world."

"But Lord," they protested, "We can't do that! We don't have the strength; we don't have the 'know-how.' We don't have the power. We don't have the courage."

"Don't worry," the Master assured them. "I won't leave you alone. I will send you a helper. I will send you strength and power. I will send the Holy Spirit to be with you always."

And then Jesus ascended into heaven, and the disciples (following his instructions) waited for the gift of the Holy Spirit. Like little children, the disciples went back to the security of the upper room to think this all through, to sort this all out, and to wait for the Holy Spirit to come. (See Matthew 28:16-20; Mark 16:14-18; Luke 24:44-49; John 20:19-23; Acts 1:1-14.)

Now think about this—picture it in your mind. Their Lord has gone. The task is squarely upon their shoulders. The disciples feel so inadequate and so scared, and now they sit and wait for this Holy Spirit to come. And they were not very good at waiting. On earlier occasions when Jesus told them to wait, they either in their impatience had done the wrong thing or in their apathy had fallen asleep. Now, here they were, waiting, and I can just imagine them grumbling and griping.

"This waiting is driving me up the wall! How long do we have to hang around here, anyway?"

"We don't know anything about this Holy Spirit. I've never *seen* any Holy Spirit. I mean, how do we know it really exists?"

"Maybe we misunderstood him. We've been here a long time and nothing has happened."

"Maybe no Holy Spirit is coming after all. Maybe it's over."

"Maybe we should just face that and accept that, and give up and go back to our old lives."

"No!" says Simon Peter. "We wait. He told us the Holy Spirit will come, and I believe him. With all my heart, I believe him."

Just at that moment they heard something, a strange sound, way off in the distance, becoming louder and louder as it moved toward them, a sound like the rush of a mighty wind, and it blew on that place. Oh, my, did it blow on that place! And they were all filled with the Holy Spirit.

As Bob Dylan later sang it, "The answer, my friend, is blowin' in the wind. The answer is blowin' in the wind." The wind of the Holy Spirit came, and they received courage and confidence and strength and new life; and through the power and presence of the Holy Spirit, they said yes to life, and they became the church of the living God on that Pentecost Day. Through the gift of the Holy Spirit, they were empowered to get up and take up the preaching, teaching, healing, caring ministry of Jesus Christ.

Some years ago, our grandson Paul was showing me what he could do on his computer. He was just four years old at the time, and already he was using a computer. He had a Tonka Toy™ CD, and he put it into the computer, and on the computer screen he was showing me how he could use a bulldozer to build highways through the desert, a snow plow to clear icy roads in the mountains, and even a helicopter to build a bridge across a canyon. It was fascinating to watch his mind work and his little hand move the computer mouse to get the results he wanted. As he continued to play his computer game, we got into a conversation that went like this. I said, "Paul, are you still enjoying school?"

"Yes, sir."

"Do you have lots of friends at school?"

"Yes, sir. I do."

"Well, tell me about Danielle. [That was his girlfriend then.] Is she still in your class?"

"Yes, sir."

Then I said, "Paul, who is your best friend?"

Paul stopped playing on his computer. He turned and looked me square in the eye, and he said, "You!"

Oh, wow! What a moment that was—a powerful moment that will stay with me forever. That look in his eyes, that tone in his voice said it all: "Gran, don't you know? *You* are my best friend!"

Now, the good news of Pentecost is that *God is our best friend.* He will always be there for us. We are not alone. God is with us, and his strength will see us through. His strength will carry us. His strength will save us.

I saw a bumper sticker the other day with a saying that fascinates me. It said, "If God has a refrigerator, your picture is on it." Because of Pentecost, because of the gift of the Holy Spirit, because of God's sustaining presence with us as Christian people, we can face the future with steady eyes and hopeful hearts. Even when things sometimes look so bleak and dreary and scary, we can live with courage and poise and grace and confidence because God is with us. Let me show you what I mean with three thoughts. Here's number one.

First of All, the Holy Spirit Enables Us to Say Yes to Life

In those critical days after the Crucifixion, I imagine that there were some hard, uncertain, discouraging moments when the disciples were tempted to throw in the towel and quit on life. We all know the feeling.

Recently, I ran across a list of commandments for living into the future. The commandments call for us to be grateful, to be committed, to celebrate life, to give and receive love. They encourage us to be tenderhearted and compassionate and accepting of ourselves and others. All the commandments in that particular list were helpful and thoughtful, but the one that really caught my eye was the one that said, "Don't mummify." I take this to mean don't quit on life and walk through your days like a mummy.

By the way, Webster defines a *mummy* as "lifeless flesh." If you've ever seen a mummy, you know that there is something physical there, there's a body there, but it is lifeless. There is no breath, no heartbeat, no vitality, no spirit, no soul, no life in a real mummy.

Sadly, some people are like that. They have become disillusioned with life. They have lost their fire, their drive, their hope, and somberly they just go through the motions. They get up in the morning, they go to work, they eat, they sleep, they exist, they endure, they watch TV—but *they are mummified.*

They have thrown in the towel. They have given up. They have quit on life. They have no zest, no joy, no spirit. They are lifeless flesh. They are all wrapped up in the clothes of death and defeat. They have forgotten how to seize the moment and celebrate life. So, they trudge, they drift, they stonewall, they tune out, they mummify. Please don't let that happen to you. Please don't drop out. God has a better plan for us than that. God has a better way. Let me show you what I mean.

Some years ago a group of hikers got lost in a cave out west. They could not figure out how to get out. It was dark, the oxygen was low, and the outlook was dismal. It looked like they were doomed to die in that cave. However, one young man in the group told everybody else to sit and rest, and he went looking for the way out. Fortunately, he found an exit route. He made his way back through the darkness and told the others the good news—he had found the way to safety. Then he led the group up and out of the cave and saved their lives. Another person in the group said later, "You can't imagine the feeling of relief and joy we felt when that young man came back for us and said, 'Follow me! I know the way out!' "

This is what the Christian gospel says to us: Here is one who knows the way to safety and life. Here is one who can deliver you. Here is one who can save you. Follow him, and you can live.

Now, there is a sad footnote to that story about the people lost in the cave, one that serves as a poignant parable for us. When that young man came back to save the people, some followed his lead while others refused to go with him. They didn't believe him, they didn't trust him, they didn't follow him. They gave up, they "mummified," they stayed in the cave, and eventually they died. Life was there for them, but they refused to accept it, and they perished. Please don't let that happen to you. Say yes to the Savior. Say yes to the Holy Spirit, and the Holy Spirit will enable you to say yes to life. That's number one.

Second, the Holy Spirit Enables Us to Say Yes to Other People

On the day of Pentecost, people from all different nations were brought together, and the Holy Spirit enabled them to communicate and to understand. The Holy Spirit brought them together. (See Acts 2:1-12.)

When the noted poet Edwin Markham reached the age of retirement, he discovered that his banker had cheated him. He was ready to retire, but he found out that his banker had stolen away much of his retirement money. Edwin Markham was heartsick. Understandably, he felt hurt and betrayed, and he became bitter. As the days passed, he became obsessed with bitterness. His bitterness became such poisonous venom within him that he could no longer write poetry. All he could do was entertain thoughts of revenge.

One day while sitting at his desk, he was thinking about this man who had so wronged him. Edwin Markham said that suddenly he felt the spirit of God sweeping over him and saying, "Markham, if you do not deal with this thing, it's going to ruin you. You cannot afford the price you are paying. You must forgive that man." Following the leading of the Holy Spirit, Edwin Markham dropped to his knees, and he prayed, "Lord, I will, and I do freely forgive that man."

Edwin Markham said, "Then a miracle occurred. The resentment was gone and the poetry began to flow once again." In fact, it was right after that moment that Edwin Markham sat down and wrote his most famous poem, "Outwitted":

> He drew a circle that shut me out—
> Heretic, rebel, a thing to flout.
> But Love and I had the wit to win:
> We drew a circle that took him in.

It is the powerful presence of the Holy Spirit that enables us to forgive like that, to love like that. The Holy Spirit enables us to say yes to life and to say yes to other people.

Third and Finally, the Holy Spirit Enables Us to Say Yes to God

The reason we can say yes to God is because God has already said yes to us. If we were to make a list of the most beloved hymns of all time, one of the hymns certain to make the list would be the gospel hymn "Just as I Am, Without One Plea." It has been called the world's greatest soul-winning hymn. That is partly due to the influence of Billy Graham and his crusades. Billy Graham walked to the altar in his conversion as a young man to the singing of that hymn, and ever since, his crusades on every continent have used it as the invitation hymn.

But the real power of the hymn is found in the one who wrote the words many years ago. Her name was Charlotte Elliott. She was born in England in 1789. When she was thirty-two years old, she suffered a rare illness that left her a permanent invalid. She sank into great despair and angry, hostile rebellion against God. The next year, her concerned father brought a minister into their home to talk with his daughter. God was with that minister that day. He said just the right words in just the right tone of voice, and suddenly the presence of God was felt powerfully in that room.

Charlotte Elliott felt the Holy Spirit touching her heart, and she gave up her rebellion against God, placing her complete trust in Jesus Christ and accepting him as her Savior. From that moment, she did an interesting thing. Until her death at age eighty-two, she always celebrated her birthday on that date, the date of her *spiritual* birth. She felt that that day she really came alive. Later, she wrote that famous hymn that is her own spiritual autobiography:

> Just as I am, without one plea,
> But that thy blood was shed for me,
> and that thou bidst me come to thee,
> O Lamb of God, I come, I come.

It's the Holy Spirit that enables us to turn things around and say yes to life, yes to other people, and yes to God.

11

From Magic-Lamp Praying to Friendship-with-God Praying

"How Do We Pray?"

Read Luke 11:1-4.

I am doing something again this year that I love to do: I am praying for every member of our church by name. Here's how it works: we send out a letter to members of our church informing them that I will be praying for them specifically in a certain month. For example, I prayed for everybody in our church whose last name starts with an A or B in January, the Cs and Ds in February, and so on.

In the letter I say, "If there is something in particular you want me to pray about, please let me know." The response has been amazing. In my study, I have on my desk two large expandable folders _stuffed_ with prayer requests. Some are general in nature, most are quite specific, all are very sincere. This incredible response to that one letter has underscored once again for me how important prayer is to us.

On the evening of September 11, 2001, after the terrorist attacks, a thousand people came to our church's sanctuary and knelt at the altar to pray. And again on that Friday after the attacks, a thousand people came to a noonday service to participate at the altar in the National Day of Prayer. That scene repeated itself all over our nation, and indeed, all over our world. In the painful wake of that horrific tragedy, people wanted and needed to be in church, people wanted and needed to pray together—another dramatic reminder of how important prayer is to us.

On the other hand, think about this. Some years ago when Leonard Griffith was pastor of the famous City Temple in London, he wrote a fascinating book entitled *Barriers to Christian Belief.* In that book he dealt with some problems that over the years have been real obstacles and stumbling blocks for people in their faith pilgrimage, specific problems that hinder people, that burden people, that frustrate and disturb people, and that keep them away from the Christian faith. One of the barriers he listed was "unanswered prayer." It does seem to be a fact of our experience that many people do get discouraged and they do give up and drop out of the faith because they feel a sense of failure in their prayer life.

This leads us to ask: How do you pray? Why pray at all? When do you pray? Is there a special formula or a sacred language that should be used? One thing is for sure, prayer must be more than a vague nod in God's direction or an emergency magical lamp to rub in a crisis. The truth is that many people give up on prayer because they never understand what prayer is. Much that passes for prayer is irrational, superstitious, and self-centered and is therefore unworthy of the pattern of prayer we find in Jesus.

How do you pray, and why? We are not the first to ask. The disciples of Jesus came to him one day and said, "Lord, teach us, teach us to pray!" Notice something here. When did the disciples ask for this? When did they make this request? Was it after Jesus gave a lecture on prayer? No. Was it after Jesus led a seminar on prayer? No. Was it after

Jesus preached a powerful sermon on prayer? No; none of these. Remember how it is recorded in Luke 11:1, "[Jesus] was praying in a certain place, and after he had finished, one of his disciples said to him, 'Lord, teach us to pray.' "

The disciples were impressed by how important Jesus' prayer life was to him. The incredible spiritual power produced in him by his prayer time—that's what got their attention. They wanted that, too.

Sometimes the disciples were slow on the uptake, but at this point they were quickly and precisely on target. They saw in Jesus the answer to this question: *How do you pray, and why?* And they learned from him (as we can) the key elements that lead to a meaningful prayer life. There are many, but let me list three of them for us to think about.

First of All, Jesus Prayed Regularly—and So Can We

Jesus took the time to pray. He made it a vital part of his daily schedule. He disciplined himself to pray regularly. From childhood, Jesus had prayed at regular intervals throughout the day, and he knew that regular times of prayer, faithfully observed, could produce the kind of vitality in one's spiritual life, the kind of dynamic in one's faith lifestyle, and the kind of depth in one's awareness of God that is just not possible in the hit-and-miss procedure that many of us use in our approach to prayer.

Let me tell you something. I know about busy schedules. I know about deadlines. I know about time pressures and stresses and demands in our frantic lifestyle. I live in that world. But I also know that when we feel we are so busy and our schedules are so hectic and the competition is so fierce and the times are so tough that we can't afford to take the time to pray, then that's the moment when we need to pray most of all; that's the moment when we can't afford *not* to take the time to pray!

Everything worthwhile takes time—regular, disciplined time. Ask any artist. Ask any musician. Ask any athlete. Ask any doctor or lawyer or minister or engineer; it takes time, effort, determination. You have to plug away at it. It doesn't come overnight, and it doesn't stay with you unless you stay with it. Maybe the same is true with prayer. Maybe it just takes a lot of practice—and you know, I think it's worth it. If Jesus felt the need to pray regularly, how much more must *we* need to pray regularly?

Second, Jesus Prayed Sensibly—and So Can We

Jesus prayed with intelligent common sense. He did not use prayer as some magical device to get selfish wishes. Hoover Rupert spoke to this when he said, "How easy it is to blurt out a desperate prayer, 'O Lord, make the brakes hold,' when we are going eighty miles an hour and suddenly face a need for a quick stop to avoid hitting another car. Not much intelligence in such a prayer, not much common sense" (Hoover Rupert, *What's Good About God*, p. 155). Or take the example where there is the student who goes into an exam praying, "Lord, I didn't study, but if you'll give me the answers, I'll do better next time."

Some time ago, I was reading an article in *Sports Illustrated* about a Major League baseball pitcher who prays that God will help him "get 'em out" and a player on an opposing team who says he prays that God will help him "get a hit." The sportswriter said, "How confusing this must be to God when they face each other!"

How senseless to see God as nothing more than a pawn to be used for our own selfish desires. How senseless to picture God as some kind of divine waiter who at our slightest whim rushes off to a heavenly kitchen then runs back with steaming portions of whatever we have asked for. How senseless to expect God to do for us what we can do for ourselves. Jesus prayed regularly, and he prayed sensibly—and so can we.

Third and Finally, Jesus Prayed Trustingly— and So Can We

"Thy will be done." That was the prayer of Jesus (Luke 11:2 KJV), and it is a prayer that we can pray in complete trust because God knows us better than we know ourselves. Like a loving parent, God knows what we need and what is good for us, better than we know.

When our grandson Paul was four-and-a-half years old, he went through a funny stage. Whenever his mother asked him to do something, such as, "Paul, please pick up your socks," or "Paul, please drink your milk," or "Paul, would you clean up your room?" Paul would snap to attention, salute, and like a boot camp private, say, "Ma'am, yes, ma'am!" And then he would march off to do what his mother had asked. Now, we had no idea where Paul learned this or how long it would last, but his mother enjoyed that stage immensely. Paul trusted her completely. He was convinced that his mom loved him, that she knew best and had his best interests at heart.

Let me ask you something: Do you trust God like that? Can you say to God, and mean it, "Thy will be done in my life"?

Someone once described prayer simply like this: "Prayer is friendship with God." That's a pretty good definition, isn't it? We can just talk to God like a trusted friend.

Some years ago, Leslie Weatherhead told a beautiful story about an elderly Scottish man who was quite ill. The minister came to see the dying man and noticed an empty chair on the opposite side of the bed. The chair was pulled up especially close to the edge of the bed. The older man said, "Let me tell you about this chair. Many years ago I found it difficult to pray, so one day I shared my problems with my pastor. He told me not to worry about kneeling or about placing myself in some pious position or about speaking in high-sounding words. Instead, he said, 'Just sit down, put a chair in front of you, and imagine God sitting there in that chair, and then just talk to him as you would talk to a trusted friend.'" The older man said, "I tried that. It worked for me and I've been doing that ever since."

Some days later, the daughter of the older man called the minister to tell him that her father had died peacefully. And then she said, "For some reason, his hand was on that empty chair on the other side of the bed. Isn't that strange?" The minister said, "Oh no, it's not strange at all. I understand perfectly. He was reaching out in trust to his best friend."

That's what prayer is. It's reaching out to God. It's reaching out in trust to our best friend and saying, "Lord, here's what's going on with me. Here's what I'd like, but Thy will be done, 'cause you are a lot smarter than I am, and I trust you with all my heart."

Jesus prayed regularly. He prayed sensibly. And he prayed trustingly. And so can we.

12

From Fear to Confidence

"THE NAME OF GOD IS
'I SHALL BE THERE'"

─────────

Read Exodus 3:1-15.

Not too long ago, our son Jeff and his family moved into
a brand new home. Jeff and his wife, Claire, who are the
proud parents of two fine boys, Dawson (age 4) and Daniel
(age 2), were delighted to discover that all around them in
their new neighborhood were young couples who also
have preschool-age children.

Recently, two little girls from across the street came over
to play with Dawson and Daniel. Dawson and Daniel were
excited because the two little girls were really cute. Four-
year-old Dawson was especially pleased because he has
something of a crush on the five-year-old girl. As soon as
they arrived, all four children ran upstairs to play in the
playroom.

Jeff said that the children were playing together so
well—no crying, no fussing, no squabbling, and no crashes.
However, after about thirty minutes or so, Jeff thought that
he had better go up to check on them. When Jeff walked
into the playroom, Dawson took one look at him and said,
"Daddy, don't you have a meeting downstairs with
Momma?"

That sounds like something a junior-high or senior-high young person might say, doesn't it? But it is also similar to what happened when Moses experienced the presence of God in the burning bush. Things were going well for Moses. He didn't want to be bothered or interrupted, so in effect he said to God, "Lord, don't you have a meeting somewhere with somebody else? Surely you don't want *me* to be the one to go face the Pharaoh and demand the release of your people. Things are going great for me. Couldn't you call on somebody else?"

This is a dangerous mission, risky business, a frightening task that God wants to lay on Moses, and Moses knows it. I mean, you don't tell Egyptian kings what to do. You don't tell Pharaohs *anything*, do you? Pharaohs do the telling, and everybody jumps to quickly obey—or else heads will roll.

Notice how Moses responds, just as we would: "Who? Me? Lord, you're not talking to *me,* are you? Of all people; why *me*? You have *got* to be kidding! I have *lots* of good excuses. I'm not a good *speaker;* I'm not *eloquent;* and besides, I'm already in big trouble back there in Egypt. And it's so peaceful here, so calm and serene. Lord, couldn't you pick someone else? I can't do this. Lord, I can't do this! Couldn't you go meet with somebody else about this?"

But God will not be put off. "Go, Moses," he says. "Set my people free. Go, and I will go with you!" Moses, still not too excited about taking on the power of Pharaoh, hedges a little more. "But Lord, by what authority? I don't have any authority. I can't just go over there and demand the release of these captives. They are going to want to know where I'm coming from and by what authority I'm speaking. Lord, who are you? Who shall I say sent me? What is your name?" And God answers, "I AM WHO I AM" (Exodus 3:14). At least, that's the way most scholars translate it.

However, the great Old Testament scholar Martin Buber said something about this toward the end of his life, something that touched my heart greatly. After studying the original Hebrew text for many years, Martin Buber said he finally came to the conclusion that we may well have mistranslated that verse. Instead of being translated that the name of God is "I AM WHO I AM," Buber believed it should instead read, "I Shall Be There."

Isn't that beautiful? The name of God is "I Shall Be There." That is God's name, and that is God's greatest promise, and that is good news. We need to wrap our arms around it and always remember that whatever we have to deal with in this life, come what may, the name of God is "I Shall Be There"!

Let me show you what I mean with three thoughts that emerge from this story of Moses in the book of Exodus.

First of All, When We Have to Face the Pharaohs of Life, We Can Remember That the Name of God Is "I Shall Be There"

Can you just imagine how Moses must have felt as he approached the Pharaoh? The Pharaoh had all the power, all the clout. This was a scary, frightening situation that Moses had to face. He had to confront and challenge one of the most powerful, most threatening, most intimidating men in the world of that time. Though perhaps not so dramatically, all of us who live in this world sometimes have to face frightening situations like that.

Let me ask you something. What are the "Pharaohs" you are facing right now? What are the frightening, scary things you are up against right now? Is it a problem at work or at home? Is it a health problem, or a financial concern?

Do you know Dean DeOvies's famous cemetery story? When Dean DeOvies was a little boy in England, he used to play in the cemetery at night. One night he accidentally fell into a newly dug grave, which was so deep that he could not get out, no matter how hard he tried. Finally, in exhaustion, he sat down in the dark corner of the grave to wait until morning. Suddenly, he heard footsteps, then whistling. (That's what people do in graveyards at night. They whistle!) It was his friend Charlie. Dean DeOvies said that his first reaction was to call out for help, but he decided to wait a while and see what would happen.

Sure enough, Charlie fell into the same grave. Dean DeOvies sat quietly and undetected in the dark corner as Charlie tried frantically to get out. After a bit, Dean DeOvies decided to have some fun, and he said loudly in a deep voice, *"You can jump all you want to, Charlie, but you'll never get out of here!"* But Charlie did! In a single bound, he went up and out of that grave as if he had wings!

Now, there is a strong point here—namely, the power of motivation. If Charlie were that motivated by fear, why can't we turn the coin over and be that strongly motivated by confidence, the confidence that comes from claiming God's most significant promise, "I shall be there"?

The claiming of that promise turned Simon the denier into Peter the Rock. It turned Saul the persecutor into Paul the missionary. It turned the weak, stammering, reluctant Moses into the powerful, eloquent, courageous Moses, the champion of Israel.

Now, we can claim that promise too. Today. Right now. In your life and mine, we can claim that promise. When we feel frightened or threatened or scared or inadequate, when we feel insecure or troubled or burdened or challenged by the frightening Pharaohs of this world, then we, like Moses, can remember with confidence that God's name is "I Shall Be There"!

This is the good news of the Bible. On page after page of the Scriptures, over and over again, we find it, God's greatest promise, that he will never desert us. He will always be there for us. Nothing can separate us from God and his love. Whatever frightening situation we have to face, we can remember with confidence that God's name is "I Shall Be There."

That's number one: when we have to face the frightening Pharaohs of life, we can remember that the name of God is "I Shall Be There"!

Second, When We Have to Wander in the Wilderness, We Can Remember That the Name of God Is "I Shall Be There"

Some years ago, a young actress named Jeanette Clift George had a wonderful dream. She wanted to take Christian theater into the marketplace. She wanted to put on plays out in the community to teach people the Christian faith, to reach people with the good news of Jesus Christ, to present good theater to the secular world that lifted up faith and family values, theater that acted out on stage the drama of redemption.

But she was wandering in the wilderness. She had no resources, no money, no theater—just a handful of young, starving actors who wanted to be a part of her dream. On faith, Jeanette and her players started rehearsing a play. A reporter came out to do a story on them, and he asked, "What's the name of your group?" Jeanette hadn't even thought of a name, but as she looked into the hungry faces of her fellow actors, she suddenly blurted out, "We are the After Dinner Players!" She said she thought, "We are all starving actors, so maybe with that name, somebody might invite us to perform after dinner, and they might give us a meal as a part of the deal."

Well, that's exactly what happened. Jeanette and her company of actors would go to big banquets in town and get a meal, and then after dinner they would provide the entertainment. Along the way their name was shortened to the A.D. Players—and you know what A.D. means, don't you? It is an abbreviation for the Latin *anno Domini*, which means "in the year of Our Lord." Today, they have their own theater (they call it, appropriately, Grace Theater), and they are the Year of Our Lord Players—the A.D.Players, which Jeanette says is the name God had in mind for them from the very beginning. Today, Jeanette says they were "wandering in the wilderness, somewhat lost, but God was there with us all along."

All God asks is for us to be faithful to the dream, to not lose heart—and he in his own good time will bring us to the promised land! When we have to face the Pharaohs of life and when we have to wander in the wilderness, we can remember with confidence that God's name is "I Shall Be There."

Third and Finally, When We Have to Face Death, Then Too (Even Then, Especially Then) We Can Remember That the Name of God Is "I Shall Be There"

Let me ask you something. Did you realize that Moses never made it to the promised land? God had foretold that Moses would not enter the promised land with the rest of the Israelites (see Deuteronomy 32:48-52), and Moses died just before they got there.

He led the people out of Egyptian bondage. He led them through the Red Sea. He led them through the wilderness. He taught them how to be God's people. But when they came to a mountain where they could look over and see the promised land, Moses, whose body was by now old and weak and worn, didn't have the strength to go on. He passed the torch to Joshua, and Joshua led the people into the land while Moses stayed behind on the mountain, alone.

Can you imagine how it felt for him to be so near but yet so far, so close to the land he had dreamed of entering and yet too old and too sick and too tired to go on. I can just imagine this conversation between Moses and God. I can hear Moses saying, "Lord, I know your plan is best, but I can't help but feel disappointed. I wanted so much to lead the people into the land. I had dreamed of that. I wanted that so badly, and now this. I'm so weak, so frail, so tired. If only I could have had a little more time."

And God answers, "Moses, Moses, you have served me well. You have done your part. It will very soon be time for you to come and live with me." Moses looks down from the mountain, and he sees the people moving forward toward the land without him, and suddenly Moses feels so alone. Moses looks up into the heavens, and quietly he says, "Are you with me, Lord? Are you with me?" And the answer comes back, "Of course I am, Moses. Of course I am."

This is the good news of our faith. When we have to face the frightening Pharaohs of life, when we have to wander in the wilderness, and when we have to face death, we can remember with confidence that the name of God is "I Shall Be There."

13

From Not Knowing the Words to Knowing the Code Words of Faith

"THE WINDTALKERS"

Read Judges 12:5-6.

A movie about World War II came out a few years ago. It's called *Windtalkers*. I haven't seen it yet, but I have read a number of reviews of this movie, and it is amazing how dramatically opinionated and divided the critics are about it. They love it or they hate it.

Some say it's too violent, too profane, too graphic, too shallow, too unrealistic, and too one-dimensional. Others say it's the greatest war movie since *Saving Private Ryan*. Well, I'll leave it to the critics to battle it out. What I'm interested in, regarding this movie, is the basic premise—Navajo Native Americans who were code talkers helping the war effort.

On December 7, 1941, the Japanese bombed Pearl Harbor. The next day, December 8, 1941, the U.S. declared war on Japan. For the next several years, U.S. forces were heavily engaged in battle throughout the Pacific, taking over islands one by one, in a slow progression toward mainland Japan. But there was a big problem. During this brutal campaign, the Japanese were continually breaking the secret codes the Americans were using, dramatically slowing U.S. progress. Something had to be done about it. So, in 1941, the U.S. military leaders came up with an ingenious plan. Navajos at opposite ends of the communication systems gave necessary messages in their native language. Navajo is a particularly difficult language to learn, if you are not born into that nation. It has been said that it takes up to ten years to learn the Navajo language. The Japanese couldn't understand the messages at all. They thought that it was some kind of secret code, and they could not break it. These Navajo messengers had a special title. They were called *windtalkers*.

To the outsider all they were saying was gibberish. The outsiders didn't understand it, couldn't comprehend it. It made no sense to them at all. But to the code talkers, to the ones who understood the words, it all made perfect sense, and they knew how to receive the message and how to respond to it. The Navajo code was the only one never broken by the Japanese and is considered to have been a key factor in winning the war.

There is a fascinating old story in the Old Testament that relates to this if we use a little poetic license. It's the story of one of the Hebrew judges. His name is Jephthah. You can find him in the twelfth chapter of the book of Judges. Let me outline the story.

Jephthah has just won a decisive victory over the Ammonites. The Ephraimites are jealous, so they come over the Jordan River to Zaphon, angry, hostile, dressed and ready for war. Jephthah and his troops severely rout the Ephraimites, and the Ephraimites who survive are scattered in the land. The surviving Ephraimite soldiers, realizing their defeat, try to get back across the Jordan River to safety, but they discover that Jephthah has set up roadblocks at all the fords of the river.

Jephthah was pretty shrewd, and he devised a plan to quickly expose the Ephraimites. When a man arrived at a ford of the Jordan and wanted to go across, he was asked, "Are you an Ephraimite?" When he replied, "No," which he obviously would say, the roadblock troops would then say to him, "If you are not an Ephraimite, then say *Shibboleth,*" which was a word meaning "ear of corn" or "flood" (but the meaning of the word is not important here). The key thing was the pronunciation because the Ephraimites could not correctly pronounce the word *Shibboleth,* and Jephthah knew this.

When an Ephraimite tried to say the word, it came out *Sibboleth.* Those who said *Sibboleth,* rather than *Shibboleth,* were executed on the spot, and according to the Old Testament story, 42,000 of them fell that day because they didn't know the code word.

This is a crude, colorful, but fascinating war story about the importance of knowing and saying the right word at the right time. Knowing the right word meant life. Not knowing it meant death. It's a primitive story to be sure, but it's also a powerful parable for our time, a parable that dramatically reminds us of how essential it is to be able to come up with the right words at the right times. Knowing the words can mean life and hope and joy. Not knowing the words can mean confusion, despair, and defeat.

Have you ever noticed how every discipline, every profession, and every group creates its own code words? Some have suggested that they do this to keep the rest of us in our place. But I think it's deeper than that. I think it has to do with an economy of speech. That is, what they have to say is so big and so crucial and so important that they want to be able to convey in a single code word or phrase a wide and dramatic range of ideas and truths that call for response and action.

For example, think of the medical world, for a moment. Go to a hospital and get on the public address system and say the words "code blue," and see what happens. If you are an outsider, that phrase means nothing, and you might just stand there twiddling your thumbs. But if you are a responsible person in that medical world, you are thrown quickly into crucial action by the sound of that significant phrase. *Code Blue, stat, EKG, cholesterol*—all are important code words for the medical society. My father died more than forty years ago. I venture to guess that he never in his lifetime heard the word *cholesterol*, but it's an important code word in health today, isn't it?

Code words are so important. The legal profession, the military, educators, psychologists, politicians, tradespeople, retailers, athletes all have their own code language to communicate messages to their group. Let me give you a test. What do these words mean: *melismatic, partita, crescendo, pianissimo, a cappella*? If you don't know, ask a musician. Those are music code words.

And with the advent of computers, we have a whole new language to learn—*hardware, software, firmware, mainframe, network, user-friendly;* these are computer code words that convey very special meanings to those who know and understand that language.

Code words are so very important. This is especially true, uniquely true I think, in the world of faith. We as Christian people are code talkers. We are the stewards of a very special and sacred language. The code words of faith mean very little to those who don't know the language. It sounds like gibberish to them. But to those who know and understand the code words, they are the source of joy, hope, life, and inspiration.

There are so many code words in our vocabulary of faith, special words like *love, forgiveness, sin, redemption, atonement, salvation, creation, covenant, resurrection,* and on and on we could go. There are so many of them. But for now let me underscore a few crucial words that I think are especially important for us to understand as we make our faith pilgrimage and as we share our faith with the world.

First, There Is **Incarnation,** *a Crucial Code Word of Faith*

The word *incarnation* literally means "in human flesh." "The Word became flesh and dwelt among us," says the writer of John's Gospel (1:14 RSV). What on earth does that mean? It means that in Jesus Christ we see the truth of God in the flesh, wrapped up in a person. It means that in Jesus Christ, we see the purpose of God acted out before our very eyes. It means that in Jesus Christ, we see the will of God expressed in the way Jesus lived in this world. He was the living flesh-and-blood example of what God is like and what God wants us to be like.

Sometimes we see a man who is totally committed to living every day in the spirit of honesty, and we say that man is "honesty personified," honesty wrapped up in a person. Or we see a woman who lives daily in the spirit of kindness, and we say that woman is "kindness personified," kindness wrapped up in a person.

In like manner, Jesus was the Word of God, the idea of God, the truth of God personified. He was life as God meant it to be, wrapped up in a person.

Let me put it another way. Imagine that you are a teacher and your class is a group of Chinese children who know absolutely no English at all. If you said to them, "Please stand up," what would they do? They would just sit there with a puzzled look on their faces because they don't know your language. If you wrote the words "Please stand up" on the blackboard, what would they do? They would just sit there with a confused expression because they can't read your language.

What would you do? Well, you would have to show them, give them an example, act it out. You would point to yourself, indicating, "Watch me." You would sit down. Then you would stand up and motion with your hands for them to stand up, and finally they would get the message because you acted it out for them.

This is what God did for us in Jesus Christ. We didn't know God's language. God gave us his message, but we couldn't comprehend it, we couldn't get it. So God had to show us. He had to act it out. He had to give us an example. So he sent Jesus into the world and said, "Here it is. Here is my truth. This is what life is supposed to be. This is what I want you to be like. Here it is, wrapped up in a person."

A few years ago, the Gallup organization conducted a survey in which people were asked to name the one person in history they would most like to spend one day with. Many of the answers were predictable, such as George Washington, Abraham Lincoln, Jackie Kennedy, and Princess Diana. Someone even wanted to spend the day with John Wayne and with Oprah. But 75 percent of the individuals interviewed named Jesus as the one person from history with whom they most wanted to spend one day. Why? Because of the Incarnation. Because in Jesus Christ, we see the truth of God personified. In him we see the truth of God acted out, wrapped up in a person. *Incarnation:* it's a key code word in the vocabulary of faith.

Second, There Is **Grace**

Grace is without question one of the most crucial code words of the Christian faith. Grace means unconditional love, love that is not earned or merited. It is love freely given, with no strings attached. Grace means loving people even when they don't deserve it and even when they don't love you back.

A few weeks ago, late at night, I was surfing the TV channels with the remote control when I came upon the award-winning movie *Driving Miss Daisy*. I couldn't help myself—I watched it again. It's a great film, and it is indeed the story of grace.

Miss Daisy is a wealthy older woman who because of her age is unable to drive her car anymore. She is not happy about that at all. Against her wishes, her son hires a man named Hoke to be her chauffeur. Miss Daisy resents this, and she resents Hoke. She makes up her mind not to like him or accept him, and she gives him a hard time. In her mind he is an intrusion into her privacy, and she thinks he can do nothing right.

He dusts the chandelier, and she fusses at him. He weeds her flower garden, and she fusses at him. He offers to put in a vegetable garden for her, and she fusses at him. He offers to drive her to the grocery store, and she fusses at him. And when she finally agrees to let him drive her to the store the first time, she complains that he is driving too fast and wasting gas, even though he is going only nineteen miles an hour in a thirty-five-miles-per-hour zone. She's giving him a hard time.

Through it all, Hoke keeps on loving her. He keeps on being kind to her. He keeps on taking care of her. And finally, his gracious spirit wins her over, and in the end, she says, in effect, "Hoke, you are the best friend I have in all the world." In that movie, Hoke is the symbol of grace and unconditional love.

The good news of our faith is that God is grace. God loves us unconditionally and unflinchingly, and he wants us to live in that spirit of grace with each other. "Amazing Grace," we sing in that beloved hymn—and when you stop to think about it, grace is indeed amazing. Let me show you what I mean.

If a totally selfish person who knew nothing of religion, nothing of Christianity, nothing of God's grace read the parable of the prodigal son, he would say that the father in the parable was foolish to forgive the prodigal and welcome him back home like that. But you and I as Christian people, as children of grace, read that story, and when we see how the father accepted the prodigal son back home with love and forgiveness, we say that's beautiful. That's wonderful. That's amazing grace. Grace is a great code word of faith, and it's an even greater spirit to live by.

Finally, Another Key Code Word of Faith Is Conversion

A member of a program for recovering alcoholics said that his process of recovery began on the day he decided to buy an exceptionally fine watch. In his words, "The watch combined a chronometer, a stopwatch, a calendar, and an astronomical observatory. It indicated the time, the days of the month, and the phases of the moon. In fact, all it lacked was hot and cold running water." He said, "Then I realized something. I realized that if this watch ever needed repair it could not be taken to just anybody, it could not be taken to an ordinary repairperson. It would need to be taken to its maker!"

That's what conversion is. It's when we realize that our lives need repair, that we are broken and mixed up and running out of control, and that the only one who can fix us is the one who made us. The hymn writer put it like this:

Have thine own way, Lord! Have thine own way!
Thou art the potter; I am the clay.
Mold me and make me after thy will,
while I am waiting, yielded and still.
("Have Thine Own Way, Lord")

Incarnation, grace, conversion: three very special code words of faith, code words that mean for us hope, life, and victory.

14

From the Fear of Death to the Promise of Eternal Life

"What Do We Believe about Eternal Life?"

Read John 14:1-7.

Once there was a man who loved acting and loved children. To blend the two, he took up the hobby of going to elementary schools to do a one-person performance as Benjamin Franklin. He would dress up like Benjamin Franklin and tell his story in the first person. It gave the children an up close and personal encounter with Benjamin Franklin and some idea of his important place in American History.

The actor loved the role and he would really get into it with wit and enthusiasm and energy. In that dramatic presentation, he would "become" Benjamin Franklin. At the conclusion of his performance, the young students would be wide-eyed and inquisitive. The actor especially loved this interaction with the children and he would take their questions and answer them with all of his thespian skills, still in the role of Benjamin Franklin. He took the usual questions from the children about the way he dressed and the way he talked and of course about his experience with the kite, But then one day, a boy raised his hand and said, "I thought you died."

The actor, staying in character, answered, "Well, you are absolutely right, I did. I died on April 17, 1790, but I came back just so I could come and visit with all of you today."

The actor was so proud of himself. He thought he had come up with a sharp answer to the question and he was quite pleased with his ability to think on his feet like that. But just then, another hand went up on the back row and a little girl asked, "When you were in heaven, did you see my mother?" The actor was stunned and taken aback by the question. He could tell by the little girl's tone of voice that she had probably just lost her mother and the question was very important to her. The actor knew he had to say something. What would you have said in that situation? The actor paused to think and silently he prayed, "O God, help me!" Then he heard himself say to the little girl, "I sure did and she was the prettiest angel in heaven."

The little girl needed to hear a resurrection story. The little girl needed affirmation of what the Bible promises— the good news of our Christian faith, the power of salvation, the promise of eternal life, that nothing, not even death, can separate us from the love of God in Christ Jesus our Lord.

Some months ago, a college student came to see me. He had come home from college because his grandfather was critically ill. He came into my office, sat down, and said, "I guess I've been fortunate. I have never experienced the death of someone close to me, but now my granddad, who had always been my hero, is dying. He doesn't have much time left. The people at the hospital say it's hopeless, but you and others here at the church have taught us about another kind of hope." Then, as only a college sophomore could say it, he added, "So, Jim, I want to hold your feet to the fire. Tell me why you believe in eternal life."

I reached over and picked up a legal pad from my desk and said, "Let's work on this together. Let's see how many reasons to believe in eternal life we can list." Actually, we came up with several, but for now let me just share three of those with you. There are many. I'm sure you will think of others, but for now let's take a look at these three.

First of All, We Remembered That the Great Christians Were Not Afraid of Death Because They Believed Strongly in Eternal Life

There is no doubt about this. The great Christians were not afraid of death. They faced it squarely, confidently, courageously. "If life is Christ," they reasoned, "then death will be more of Christ, and it will not be death at all, but entrance into a larger and deeper dimension of life with God." The great Christians have all been very sure of this. History records it over and over again.

On Sunday, April 8, 1945, Dietrich Bonhoeffer was executed by Nazi soldiers. He had been leading a worship service for his fellow prisoners in a World War II death camp. Just as he finished his last prayer, the door flew open, and two guards stepped inside. One of them shouted, "Prisoner Bonhoeffer! Come with us!" Everyone knew what that meant. Bonhoeffer was to be executed; he was to die. As Bonhoeffer walked out toward the gallows, he said to his fellow prisoners, "This is the end, [but] for me the beginning of life."

Ignatius, the Bishop of Antioch in the early church, said as he was led to the arena to be thrown to the lions, "Grant me no more than to be a sacrifice for God. . . . I would rather die and get to Jesus Christ, than reign over the ends of the earth."

Polycarp, the Bishop of Smyrna, was burned at the stake in the middle of the second century because he would not curse Christ and bow down to Caesar. Polycarp said of his Lord, "Eighty-six years I have served him, and he never did me any wrong. How can I blaspheme my King who saved me?" Then as he died at the stake, he said a prayer of thanksgiving to God for the privilege of dying for the faith.

Susanna Wesley, mother of nineteen children, including John and Charles Wesley, on her deathbed called her children and their families to her side and said, "Children, as soon as I am released, sing a psalm of praise to God."

Then John Wesley's famous last words were words of great faith: "The best of all is, God is with us."

And the apostle Paul, as he faced death, spoke to his Philippian friends with a heart overflowing with joy, "Rejoice in the Lord always; again I will say, Rejoice" (Philippians 4:4); "for to me to live is Christ, and to die is gain" (Philippians 1:21 RSV).

Now, why did these great Christians, and millions and millions of Christians who came along after them, believe unwaveringly, unflinchingly in eternal life? Why were they unafraid of death? Where did they get such strength and serenity and confidence? You know the answer to that, don't you? They got it from Jesus. And that brings us to point number two.

First, we remembered that the great Christians were not afraid of death because they believed in eternal life.

Second, We Remembered What Jesus Taught Us About Life After Death

Jesus not only conquered death through his resurrection, he also taught us that there is life after death for us, and he told us that he would go there and prepare a place for us, that we might be with him. I want you to think with me for a moment about that word, *place.*

Sometimes we use that word in a bad way: "Keep 'em in their place!" But 99 percent of the time it is a good and wonderful word. Dr. Fred Craddock expresses it like this:

> I am talking about the word "place." Place. The children ran all through this new little house, a bath and five rooms built by volunteers with Habitat for Humanity. That woman and those three little girls stood there, that woman's eyes brimming with tears and the children running into each room and back then pulling at her skirt. "Mama, is this our place? Mama, is this our place?" Off they'd run and back and she'd say "Yes, yes, yes. This is going to be our place." Look at their eyes, really look at their eyes. I'm talking about the word, "place." . . . I was coming out of Cartecay Creek after another unsuccessful day of trout fishing. A man and woman drove up and got out of their car. I said, "Going to fish?" He said, "No." They opened the trunk and got out a couple of those little flexi-chairs, folding chairs. I said, "Oh, you going to have a picnic?" He said, "No." Then, they put the chairs out in front of the car and sat there.
>
> Well, I was ready to go but couldn't stand it, of course, so I said, "What're you doing?" He said, "I'm a minister in The United Methodist Church. I'm going to retire in two years. We've lived over forty years in the churches' houses, so I bought an acre here along the creek . . . and we're going to have a place of our own." I'm talking about "place." You have to have that word to understand the Bible. (*Craddock Stories*, pp. 85-86)

Isn't it beautiful when you think of the word *place* like that? I believe in eternal life because Jesus told us about it, and he also told us that he was going ahead to prepare a special place for us there.

But also, don't miss this. Do you remember how when Jesus was on the cross, just shortly before he breathed his last breath, he prayed a beautiful prayer: "Father, into thy hands I commend my spirit" (Luke 23:46 KJV)? Did you know that this probably was not the first time Jesus had prayed this prayer, "Father, into thy hands I commend my spirit"? He had likely prayed it hundreds of times as a child because, you see, this was the bedtime prayer taught to little children during biblical times. It was the first-century version of "Now, I lay me down to sleep, I pray the Lord my soul to keep." *Father, I'm about to go to sleep now, so into Thy hands I commend my spirit. I'm going to sleep now, Father. I know you are here to watch over me, and I know you will be near when I wake up.*

It was the prayer of total and complete trust. It was the prayer of total and complete confidence. It was the prayer Jesus prayed on the cross just before he died. And it is the prayer you and I can pray daily because we know that we can trust God, because we know that God has the power to turn the agony of Good Friday into the ecstasy of Easter Sunday, because we know that God has the power to take the cross (the emblem of suffering and shame) and turn it into the greatest symbol of victory this world has ever known.

As the gospel hymn writer put it, "We know not what the future holds, but we know who holds the future." The point is clear: Jesus not only told us about eternal life, he not only told us that he would go before us to prepare a place for us there, but also, in the greatest crisis moment of his life, as he endured the pain of the cross and as he died on the cross for our sins, he wrapped his arms confidently around this belief in eternal life and prayed, "Father, into Thy hands I commend my spirit." And one more thing— Jesus also showed us dramatically and powerfully through his resurrection that there is indeed life after death.

As that young college student and I made our list of why we believe in eternal life, first, we remembered how the great Christians were not afraid of death because they believed in eternal life; and second, we remembered what Jesus taught us about life after death.

Third and Finally, We Remembered the Bible's Greatest Promise: That God Loves Us and He Is with Us on Both Sides of the Grave

Whether we live or whether we die, we belong to God, and nothing—nothing—can separate us from God, not even death. For you see, death is not really death at all for the Christian. It's just a door that we label death, which we pass through to enter into a new and larger dimension of life with God.

Now, I could quote Jesus here, or the apostle Paul, but for the moment let me go another route and ask you to consider carefully the words of a great scientist. Dr. Wernher von Braun once spoke on the subject "Why I Believe in Immortality," and he said this:

> In our modern world, many people seem to feel that science has somehow made the "religious idea" (of immortality) untimely or old fashioned.
>
> But I think science has a real surprise for the skeptics. Science, for instance, tells us that nothing in nature, not even the tiniest particle, can disappear without a trace.
>
> Think about that for a moment. Once you do, your thoughts about life will never be the same.
>
> Science has found that nothing can disappear without a trace. Nature does not know extinction. All it knows is transformation!
>
> Now, if God applies this fundamental principle to the most minute and insignificant parts of His universe, doesn't it make sense to assume that He applies it also to the masterpiece of His creation—the human soul? I think it does. And everything science has taught me—and continues to teach me—strengthens my belief in the continuity of our spiritual existence after death. Nothing disappears without a trace. (*The Third Book of Words to Live By,* ed. William Nichols [New York: Simon & Schuster, 1962], p. 132)

When someone we love dies, or when we face our own death, we need to remember that. Remember that God loves us and that God is on both sides of the grave, and nothing can separate us from him. God is there, and that's really all we need to know.

Sometimes when people ask, "What is heaven like?" I feel a little like that five-year-old kindergartner who answered that question by saying, "I don't know, I ain't dead yet." Now that answer is not nearly as childish as it seems. It's really a futile exercise in supposition to try to imagine the exact nature of the hereafter. All we need to know is, God is there.

John Baillie once told a story about this that rang true for me. He told about an old country doctor who made his rounds in a horse-drawn carriage. The doctor's dog would go along with him. One day the doctor went to a home to visit one of his patients, a man critically ill. "How am I, doctor?" the man asked. The doctor replied, "It doesn't look good." Both men were quiet for a while.

Then the man said, "What's it like to die, doctor?" The old doctor sat there trying to think of some words of comfort to offer the man. Suddenly, the answer came from a scratching at the door. The doctor said, "Do you hear that? That's my dog. He's never been in this house before. He has no idea of what's on the other side of that door. He only knows one thing. He knows his master is in here. And because of that, he knows that everything is all right."

"Now," said the doctor, "Death is like that. We've never been there, and we don't know what's on the other side of the door. But we know our Master is there, and that's all we really need to know, because since he is there, we can be confident that everything is all right."

God loves us. He cares for us. He has conquered death. He has gone before us. He has prepared a place for us, and he is there. And that's all we really need to know.

15

From Trust in Self to Trust in God

"CAN WE REALLY CHANGE?"

─────────

Read Galatians 1:11-24.

It was 1:00 A.M. on Christmas Day. I was still at the church. About an hour earlier, we had finished the late-night Christmas Eve candlelighting service, the seventh full service of the day. I felt pleasantly tired but still exhilarated by the thousands of people who had come and participated joyfully in Christmas Eve at St. Luke's. I prayerfully stood in the sanctuary for a few moments, looking at the beautiful sights and symbols of Christmas that decorated the room, reflecting on our celebration of this sacred season and feeling the mellow afterglow that inevitably follows Christmas Eve.

I walked back to my office. The church, which only moments before had been filled with excited people, was now virtually empty. Things were as quiet as they ever get at St. Luke's. In my office, I opened my Christmas file to add what would soon be memorabilia from Christmas 2000. As I thumbed through the file, I found some old letters to Santa that had been written by our five-year-olds some years ago. These had been written in Sunday school, and I had kept them in my Christmas folder. I read through them and was so impressed and inspired by the love and thoughtfulness reflected in these letters. These are actual letters to Santa written by some of our church's five-year-old children.

> Dear Santa, I wish all the children in the world would get presents. Love, Stacie
> Dear Santa, I wish the whole world was happy. Love, Tristan
> Dear Santa, I wish you would bring something for the poor people. Love, Steffan
> Dear Santa, I wish you would bring everyone in our class a pet to love. Love, Will
> Dear Santa, A big stocking filled with candy canes for the whole world is what I wish for. Love, Claire
> Dear Santa, I wish for enough food to feed the whole world. Love, Jonathan
> Dear Santa, Please bring us peace, love, and no more war. Love, Terry

These letters touched me, not only because of their caring sensitivity, but also because of the recurring theme and thought in the minds of these children, the thought that things can be changed and made better.

With that in mind, let me share with you another letter. This letter was placed in the campus newspaper at Kent State University, a letter from a college student to his father. It read like this:

Dear Dad,

> Last time I was home, you told me I was too young for speaking my opinion on gradual proposals for change.
> My generation holds in contempt the colossal social, conomical, and political blunders perpetuated by your generation . . . something must change! At least we, the new generation, are beginning to think through these things.

And in our struggle, we do ask for your cooperation, realizing that our youthful ambition, coupled with your aged perspective, might together solve the riddle. Well, how about it, Dad?

Here we have a letter from a college student to his father, calling for change. Now, let me ask you something. When do you think that letter was written? In the nineties? In the eighties? Or the seventies, or in the volatile sixties? Or maybe just last year? Well, actually, it was written in 1934! The college student who wrote it is now a retired professor of journalism at Ohio State University. Like those five-year-olds writing to Santa, he too, though in a more dramatic way, was calling for change. He too wanted to make things better.

But the question is, *Can we?* Is it really possible to change? As the prophet Jeremiah put it over 2,000 years ago, can a leopard change its spots (see Jeremiah 13:23)? In other words, can a person change his or her basic nature? Can the cruel become kind? Can the vengeful become forgiving? Can the cowardly become courageous? Can the weak become strong? Can the world be made better? Can people change, really?

It's an important question, isn't it? Our world is not what we want it to be. In our personal lives, we are not all we could be. That's why at the beginning of each new year, we make resolutions. We resolve to do better and to *be* better. But, is there any hope? Can we change?

Albert Einstein once said that "it is easier to denature plutonium than it is to denature the evil spirit of man." Will Rogers once said, tongue in cheek, "You can't say that civilization doesn't advance. In every war they kill you in a new way."

And then remember Jack Paar's classic line: "Looking back, my life seems like one long obstacle race, with me as its chief obstacle."

Or how about the line that's connected with the classic comic strip character Pogo: "We have met the enemy and he is us." Many of us can relate to that, can't we?

Well, what do you think? Is it really possible to change? The answer is yes. Of course. Absolutely! With God's help, we can change. With God's help, we can be made better. History documents it. Millions of people have experienced dramatic change in their lives. They have been redeemed, converted, turned around. We see it in the Scripture lesson.

Remember how the apostle Paul writes to the Galatians and describes his own experience. He says, in effect, "You have heard of my former life . . . how I persecuted the church of God violently and tried to destroy it. But then God called me by his grace and later it was said, 'He who once persecuted us is now preaching the faith he once tried to destroy' " (Galatians 1:13, 15, 23, paraphrased).

Talk about change! Read 1 Corinthians 13, the "Love Chapter," and try to imagine that the man who wrote those beautiful words, the apostle Paul, was the same man who earlier had bitterly and violently persecuted people who disagreed with him. It's one of the most dramatic conversions of all time. But the good news is that change is a wondrous possibility for all of us. We can, with the help of God, realize our dreams and remedy our defects.

Now, to get to specifics, let me give you three basic steps that can lead to change—three very simple, very practical essentials that have to be present for change to take place in our lives.

First, There Must Be a Desire—an Intense Desire— to Change

Do we really want to change? Have we really made up our minds to change? Are we truly willing to pay the price that it requires?

King Duncan of Knoxville, Tennessee, likes to tell the humorous story about two Chicago men who had never been out of the city and who decided that they had just about "had it" with urban living. So they bought a ranch down in Texas. They decided they were going to live off the land as their ancestors had done.

The first thing they decided they needed in order to ranch was a mule. So they went to a neighboring rancher and asked him if he had a mule to sell. The rancher answered, "No, I'm afraid not." They were disappointed, but they decided to stand around and visit with the rancher for a few moments. One of the men saw some watermelons stacked against the barn and asked the rancher, "What are those?" The rancher, seeing that they were hopeless city slickers, decided to have some fun. "Oh," he answered, "those are mule eggs." The two city slickers were enthralled. "Mule eggs?" They asked. "Yes, mule eggs," the rancher answered. "You take one of those big green eggs home and wait for it to hatch, and you'll have a mule."

The Chicagoans were overjoyed at this, and they offered to buy one of those mule eggs. They agreed on a fair price, put one of those watermelons in the back of their pickup truck, and headed down the bumpy country road toward their own ranch. But suddenly they hit an especially treacherous bump, and the watermelon bounced out of the pickup truck, hit the road, and burst open. Seeing in his rearview mirror what had happened, the driver turned his truck around and drove back to retrieve his mule egg.

Meanwhile, a big old Texas jackrabbit was hopping by, and he saw this watermelon burst in the road, and he hopped over to it. The jackrabbit was standing in the middle of that watermelon, getting ready to feast, when the two city slickers drove up. Seeing their mule egg burst open and the long-eared creature in the middle of it, one of the men shouted, "Look at that! Look at that! Our mule egg has hatched!"

But then, the jackrabbit took off, with the city slickers in hot pursuit. They chased him and chased him but finally could go no further, and they wearily fell to the ground, gasping for air while the jackrabbit sped off into the distance. Raising up on his elbow, one of the men said to the other, "Well, I guess we lost our mule." The other man nodded grimly. "Yeah, but you know," he said, "I'm not sure I wanted to plow that fast anyway!"

Well, that is the real question when we come to the matter of changing our lives, isn't it: Do we want to plow that fast? In other words, do we really want to change? Do we want to pay the price and make the sacrifices involved? Whether it's changing our diet to lose weight or accepting Christ as Lord and Savior of our lives, whether it's committing ourselves to better church attendance or more Bible study or serving God better or being a kinder, more compassionate person, the key thing is to want to, to make up our minds, to have a real desire to change.

There must be a genuine desire to change. That's number one.

Second, We Need Divine Help to Change

That is, we need divine power, a power that is not our own, a power that comes only from God. That's our hope. We can't do it by ourselves, but God has the power to change us. The apostle Paul knew that dynamic power. What happened to him on the Damascus road was so powerful that he couldn't even find the words to adequately describe it. He just knew that God had exploded into his life, that God had a job for him, and that he could never be the same again. The power of God made him a changed man.

Have you heard about the two ministers' wives who sat mending their husbands' pants? One of them said to the other, "My John—he is so discouraged in his church work. He feels overworked and unappreciated. Nothing seems to go right for him. He is seriously considering quitting." The other replied, "Why, my husband is just the opposite. He is so enthused, so thrilled. It seems the Lord is closer to him than ever." A hushed silence fell as they continued to mend the trousers—one patching the knees, and the other patching the seat.

If change is to come for us, first, we need the desire; and second, we need divine help.

Third and Finally, in Order to Change, We Need Daring

We have to take a risk; we have to dare to take that first step. Getting started, daring to start, is the hardest part.

In the *New York* magazine some time ago was a cartoon entitled "Nanook Goes South." The first frame shows Nanook in the cold, frigid North, wearing his heavy parka. The second frame shows Nanook in the same outfit in the sunny South. He is sweating profusely, boiling in his parka. The caption reads, "Old habits die hard!"

Old habits do die hard, but they will indeed die if we will dare to take the first step. Some time ago, the late columnist Ann Landers shared something she had received from an anonymous source that speaks to this. It is entitled "The Dilemma":

To laugh is to risk appearing a fool.
To weep is to risk appearing sentimental.
To reach out for another is to risk involvement.
To expose feelings is to risk rejection.
To place your dreams before a crowd is to risk ridicule.
To love is to risk not being loved in return.
To go forward in the face of overwhelming odds is to risk
    failure.

But risks must be taken because the greatest hazard in life is to risk nothing.

The person who risks nothing, does nothing, has nothing, is nothing.

He may avoid suffering and sorrow, but he cannot learn, feel, change, grow, or love.

Chained by his certitudes, he is a slave—he has forfeited his freedom.

Only a person who takes risks is free.

We can change. The formula is simple. There must be a desire. There must be divine help. And there must be daring. But it can happen. By the grace of God and through the power of Christ, we can change, we can become a new person, we can be made better. It can happen because if we're going the wrong way, God allows us and empowers us to turn around.

Suggestions for Leading a Study of *If You're Going the Wrong Way . . .* Turn Around!

John D. Schroeder

This book by James W. Moore shows how God encourages and empowers turnarounds in life, giving people a new start by giving them a new sense of direction and meaning. To assist you in facilitating a discussion group, this study guide was created to help make this experience beneficial for both you and members of your group. Here are some thoughts on how you can help your group:

1. Distribute the book to participants before your first meeting and request that they read the introduction before coming to class. You may want to limit the size of your group to increase participation.
2. Begin your sessions on time. Your participants will appreciate your promptness. You may wish to begin your first session with introductions and a brief get-acquainted time. Start each session by reading aloud the snapshot summary of the chapter for the day.
3. Select discussion questions and activities in advance. Note that the first question is a general question designed to get discussion going. The last question is designed to summarize the discussion. Feel free to change the order of the listed questions and to create your own questions. Allow a set amount of time for the questions and activities.

4. Remind your participants that all questions are valid as part of the learning process. Encourage their participation in discussion by saying that there are no wrong answers and that all input will be appreciated. Invite participants to share their thoughts, personal stories, and ideas as their comfort level allows.

5. Some questions may be more difficult to answer than others. If you ask a question and no one responds, begin the discussion by venturing an answer yourself. Then ask for comments and other answers. Remember that some questions may have multiple answers.

6. Ask the question "Why?" or "Why do you believe that?" to help continue a discussion and give it greater depth.

7. Give everyone a chance to talk. Keep the conversation moving. Occasionally you may want to direct a question to a specific person who has been quiet. "Do you have anything to add?" is a good follow-up question to ask another person. If the topic of conversation gets offtrack, move ahead by asking the next question in your study guide.

8. Before moving from questions to activities, ask group members if they have any questions that have not been answered. Remember that as a leader, you do not have to know all the answers. Some answers may come from group members. Other answers may even need a bit of research. Your job is to keep the discussion moving and to encourage participation.

9. Review the activity in advance. Feel free to modify it or to create your own activity. Encourage participants to try the "at home" activity.

10. Following the conclusion of the activity, close with a brief prayer, praying either the printed prayer from the study guide or a prayer of your own. If your group desires, pause for individual prayer petitions.
11. Be grateful and supportive. Thank group members for their ideas and participation.
12. You are not expected to be a perfect leader. Just do the best you can by focusing on the participants and the lesson. God will help you lead this group.
13. Enjoy your time together!

Suggestions for Participants

1. What you will get out of this study will be in direct proportion to your involvement. Be an active participant!
2. Please make it a point to attend all sessions and to arrive on time so that you can receive the greatest benefit.
3. Read the chapter and review the study guide questions prior to the meeting. You may want to jot down questions you have from the reading, and also answers to some of the study guide questions.
4. Be supportive and appreciative of your group leader as well as the other members of your group. You are on a journey together.
5. Your participation is encouraged. Feel free to share your thoughts about the material being discussed.
6. Pray for your group and your leader.

Introduction: If You're Going the Wrong Way . . . Turn Around!

Snapshot Summary

The introduction to this book shows how God can help us make a turnaround from defeat, wrong priorities, and sin.

Reflection/Discussion Questions

1. What interests you in this topic? Share what you hope to gain from reading this book and participating in this study.
2. Why is an immediate turnaround often a better strategy than slowly cutting back or making a gradual change? Give an example of when a quick turnaround is best.
3. Share a time when you needed to make a turnaround. What motivated your desire to change?
4. What are some common danger signs that you are headed in the wrong direction?
5. List some ways in which God can turn a defeat into a victory.
6. Share a time when you realized your priorities were mixed up. What did you do to correct the situation?
7. Why are we so easily duped into sin?
8. List some reasons why it is dangerous to remain on the wrong course.
9. Compare what it might cost to make a turnaround to the potential benefits of a turnaround.
10. How can defeat be a blessing?

Activities

As a group: Use the Bible to locate stories of people who made successful turnarounds.

At home: Meditate this week on what area or areas of your life may need a turnaround.

Prayer: *Dear God, thank you for the opportunity to have a fresh start. Help us in our daily struggles, and remind us of your love and presence. Amen.*

Chapter 1: From Talking About the Cross to Taking Up the Cross: "It's Not Enough to Be Great on Paper"

Snapshot Summary

This chapter explores sacrificial service and what it means to be an authentic Christian.

Reflection/Discussion Questions

1. What insights did you receive from this chapter?
2. Give an example from your life experience or your recollection of something that looked good on paper, but in reality was not so good.
3. What does it mean to be a follower of Christ? Can you tell by appearances who is a Christian? Explain why appearances can be deceiving.
4. According to the author, what did Jesus feel was wrong with the religious leaders of his day?
5. What is "active love," and what does it symbolize?
6. What is often the key question in Jesus' parables, and why is it an important issue?
7. How did Jesus model what it means to be a servant?
8. Share a time when you were tempted to be selfish, but opted to be a servant instead. What motivated you to serve?
9. What does the sign of the cross signify?
10. What does it mean to be gracious? Give an example of a gracious person you know.

Activities

As a group: Plan a future group event in which the members of your group will minister to others. Brainstorm ideas. Select one event and set a date for it.

At home: Make a list of ways you can be an authentic Christian at home, and meditate on putting these ideas into practice.

Prayer: *Dear God, thank you for the opportunity to serve others. Help us take up your cross each day and be a witness in the world to your love. Amen.*

Chapter 2: From Old Life to New Life: "Some Things Just Need to Be Thrown Away"

Snapshot Summary

This chapter encourages us to make new beginnings by throwing away attitudes and actions that can harm us.

Reflection/Discussion Questions

1. What point was Jesus trying to get across in Matthew 5:30?
2. List and discuss the benefits of making a clean sweep in your life periodically.
3. Why do we sometimes keep things in our lives that are harmful?
4. Why is it dangerous to be selfish?
5. List the different variations of self-centeredness, as mentioned by the author, along with some examples.

6. Share a time when you were persistent and did not give in to defeat.
7. In your own words, explain the meaning of ill will and its dangers.
8. If you could get rid of one habit today, what would it be, and why?
9. What needs to be done to take a leap of faith from an old life to a new one?
10. What key learning from this chapter will you most reflect on in your personal life today? This week?

Activities

As a group: Today is a brand new day and a new beginning. Mark the occasion by creating a personal daily calendar for the next several days. Include new goals and messages of encouragement.

At home: As you drive your car or ride the bus this week, remind yourself when you turn a corner that you are going in God's direction.

Prayer: *Dear God, you give us new life and abundant life. Help us throw away the old and harmful things in our lives and start anew. Amen.*

Chapter 3: From the Quick Fix to the Deep Commitment: "Good Things That Are Here to Stay Don't Get Done in Just One Day"

Snapshot Summary

This chapter shows the importance of making a total commitment to prayer, the church, and studying the Scriptures.

Reflection/Discussion Questions

1. Why does a quick fix often fail to work? What is sometimes missing?
2. Share a time when you tried to use a quick fix and found it lacking.
3. In what ways are we often like the rich young ruler who came to Jesus?
4. What often scares people away from making a deep, total commitment?
5. Why is it costly to be a disciple? List some of the costs of following Jesus.
6. Discuss or list and reflect on the ingredients of a meaningful prayer life.
7. What does it take to discover the treasures that are within the Bible?
8. How can the Bible change your life? List some major ways.
9. Why is it important to become a real, committed church person? How do you become one?
10. Share a commitment you made that has been beneficial to you or others.

Activities

As a group: Select a topic of a social problem (such as homelessness) and create two lists. Put quick fixes on the first list, and put what is really needed to fix the problem on the second list.

At home: Reflect on what area of your life needs a deeper commitment. Come up with an action plan and take the first step this week.

Prayer: *Dear God, you desire total commitment from us. Grant us the strength to make that commitment and to take action on what we know needs to be done. Amen.*

Chapter 4: From Selfish Ambition to Humble Service: "The Meaning of Greatness"

Snapshot Summary

This chapter offers encouragement to use ambition for the good of others instead of for personal gain.

Reflection/Discussion Questions

1. Discuss or list and reflect on the good things about being an ambitious person.
2. What lessons can be learned from the story in Matthew 20:20-28 about service and greatness?
3. How do you know if your own ambition is good or bad?
4. Share a time when you were ambitious for the wrong reason.
5. Give some examples of good ambitions.
6. In your own words, explain what it means to be arrogant. How does arrogance differ from confidence?
7. What are the dangers of being adversarial? What are the dangers of being apathetic?
8. Who gets hurt by selfish, blind ambition? Give some examples.
9. When you were growing up, who showed you what it means to be a servant?
10. What key learning from this chapter will you most reflect on in your personal life today? This week?

Activities

As a group: Use newspapers and magazines to locate examples of blind, selfish ambition, as well as examples of ambition to be a servant.

At home: Write down your reflections on ways in which you see yourself as ambitious, or why you feel you lack ambition. Carefully think about ways to improve or focus your ambition so that you may better serve others.

Prayer: *Dear God, we can use our talents for good or bad causes. Help us to make the right choices and to be ambitious servants of others. Amen.*

Chapter 5: From Self-centeredness to Christ-centeredness: "Lord, Help Me to Live for Others, That I May Live Like Thee"

Snapshot Summary

This chapter offers encouragement to love others and focus on Christ.

Reflection/Discussion Questions

1. Explain what it means to be Christ-centered.
2. Name a person who taught you about love, generosity, and hospitality, and give an example of an action that touched your life.
3. How has loving others added joy to your life?
4. What's the difference between "love" and "Christlike love"?
5. Give an example of how loving others gives life a purpose.
6. How does being self-centered hurt ourselves and others? Give some examples.
7. How do you go from being self-centered to Christ-centered?
8. List some words and actions that show that the love of God is alive in us.
9. To love like Christ means to have a love for all people. How easy or how difficult is it to love

the members of your family? Your friends?
Someone who has wronged you? How can we
have love for people we've never met?

10. Compare the costs and the benefits of loving
others.

Activities

As a group: Use the Bible to locate examples of how Jesus
showed love for others.

At home: Reflect on the love of Christ this week. Focus on
others rather than yourself.

Prayer: *Dear God, thank you for giving us the opportunity to
minister to others. Help us give generously of our time and our talents to meet the needs of those who are poor, those who are sick,
those who are lonely, and all who need our help. Amen.*

Chapter 6: From Emptiness to Zestful Living: "A Prescription for Meaningful Life"

Snapshot Summary

This chapter shows how a commitment to Christ adds
zest and meaning to life.

Reflection/Discussion Questions

1. What new insights did you receive from this
chapter?

2. According to the author, what did Paul mean
when he said that his body bears the marks of
Christ?

3. Describe what living a meaningful life means to
you.

4. How can people tell a Christian from a non-
Christian?

5. Why is trust in God a key to life?
6. Share how your faith in Christ has helped you cope with life's problems.
7. Explain what it means to have "a self you can live with" and how you obtain this state of being.
8. Share a time in your life when you discovered the importance of integrity.
9. Discuss or list and reflect on ways that we learn to love others.
10. How has Christ's love changed your life?

Activities

As a group: Create two lists. The first list should contain the ingredients of a meaningful life. The second list should contain ingredients of an empty life. Compare the two lists.

At home: Take a personal inventory this week of the good and bad traits in your life. List traits you want to add and those you want to subtract. Reflect on these, and ask God to give you guidance in making choices about your life.

Prayer: *Dear God, help us always remember that a meaningful life begins with a committed relationship with you. Amen.*

Chapter 7: From Silly Fretting to Creative Worrying: *"How to Improve Your Worrying"*

Snapshot Summary

This chapter shows us that while we can't stop worrying, we can learn to put our worry to work in a positive way.

Reflection/Discussion Questions

1. According to the author, why can't we stop worrying? How is worry energy productive?
2. Why do some people worry more than others?
3. Explain the difference between "creative worry" and "silly fretting."
4. How can silly fretting harm your life?
5. What do you worry about most? Has worrying about something ever helped you? Explain.
6. Do you think you worry more or less as you have grown older? Why?
7. What advice does Jesus give about worrying?
8. How can prayer help you manage your worries?
9. List some challenges that really matter where creative worry may be helpful.
10. How can worries bring you closer to God?

Activities

As a group: Ask each person in the group to individually write down his or her top five (or top ten) list of what people worry about the most. Compare lists to see how much they differ or agree.

At home: Make a list of your worries, and then turn those worries over to God in prayer.

Prayer: *Dear God, we worry too much. And what is worse, often we worry about things that are not that important. Enable us to put our worry energy to work in a positive way, and help us turn our troubles over to you. Amen.*

145

Chapter 8: From the Good Fridays of the World to the Easter Sundays of the World: "We Too Can Be Resurrected!"

Snapshot Summary

This chapter reminds us of the power of Easter, and how God can redeem anyone and anything.

Reflection/Discussion Questions

1. What new insights about Easter did you receive from this chapter?
2. What sometimes causes people to miss the miracle of Easter?
3. God has the power to redeem. What does that mean for us today?
4. Share a favorite Easter memory. Who taught you about Easter and its meaning?
5. God can redeem events. Why is this important to remember? What impact and meaning does it have for us?
6. Share a time when God redeemed an event for you and brought good out of a bad situation.
7. Discuss how the symbol of the cross has been redeemed. What did it represent before and after Easter?
8. Share an example of redemption you have experienced or observed.
9. What do we need to do in order to be redeemed by God?
10. What key learning from this chapter will you most reflect on in your personal life today? This week?

Activities

As a group: Discuss or list and reflect on ways that you can celebrate the true meaning of Easter. Share some of your family traditions and activities related to Easter.

At home: Reflect on God's power to redeem and resurrect. Consider what opportunities to turn around God is offering you.

Prayer: *Dear God, thank you that the power of Easter sustains us every day of our lives. Easter is a daily event, as you constantly resurrect and redeem. Help us remember that your power is available to all who believe. Amen.*

Chapter 9: From Doubt to Faith: "Good News for the Doubting Thomases of the World"

Snapshot Summary

This chapter looks at what encourages and discourages us from living a life of faith in Christ.

Reflection/Discussion Questions

1. In what ways can you identify with "Doubting" Thomas?
2. List some reasons why people lack faith in God at certain times. What is the difference between an "Angry Doubter" and an "Honest Doubter"?
3. Share a time when you doubted something. Why did you doubt? Were you right or wrong about it?
4. Do you think a certain amount of doubt is healthy? Explain your answer.
5. Discuss or list and reflect on things that build faith. What turns doubt to faith?

6. Why do "dropouts" have trouble believing?
7. What role has the church played in increasing your faith?
8. Give some examples of truths that can't be documented. What can't you see, yet you believe exists?
9. Share your views on the meaning of the statement, "Death is not the end of life." What does the Bible tell us about life after death?
10. What key learning from this chapter will you most reflect on in your personal life today? This week?

Activities

As a group: Use the Bible to locate examples in which faith overcame doubt.

At home: Reflect and meditate this week on your doubts. Think about the reasons why you doubt. Try to evaluate whether your doubt is serving you well or doing you harm.

Prayer: *Dear God, we thank you that faith can triumph over our doubts. Strengthen our faith in you, and help us build up and encourage others in their faith. Amen.*

Chapter 10: From Fretfulness to Courage: "The Answer, My Friend, Is Blowin' in the Wind"

Snapshot Summary

This chapter explores the power of the Holy Spirit and how it can help us turn around in life.

Reflection/Discussion Questions

1. What is the Holy Spirit, and how does it work within us and help us?
2. Who sent the Holy Spirit to the disciples, and why?
3. Share a time of fear or of courage in your life.
4. What does the author tell us is the good news of Pentecost?
5. Give an example of how the Holy Spirit helps us say yes to life.
6. Why is it important to say yes to other people? Share a time you found the strength to do that.
7. What doors are opened when we say yes to God?
8. How does fear harm us and limit our potential?
9. Share a time when you felt the presence of God or when God helped you have courage.
10. What key learning from this chapter will you most reflect on in your personal life today? This week?

Activities

As a group: The Holy Spirit is always with us. As a reminder, draw a symbol of the Holy Spirit to carry with you in your purse or wallet. Explain your symbol to the members of your group.

At home: This week, focus on having courage, and look for ways to say "yes" to life.

Prayer: *Dear God, we thank you for the gifts of the Holy Spirit. Grant us the power and presence of the Holy Spirit this week as we strive to do your will and to serve others. Help us to be empowered to take up the ministry of Christ. Amen.*

Chapter 11: From Magic-Lamp Praying to Friendship-with-God Praying: "How Do We Pray?"

Snapshot Summary

This chapter explores the power of praying as Jesus did—regularly, sensibly, and trustingly.

Reflection/Discussion Questions

1. How have your prayers and manner of praying changed or remained the same over the years?
2. Share a memorable prayer experience in which people prayed for you or where God answered one of your prayers.
3. Why did Jesus pray regularly? How did he benefit from regular prayer, and how can we do the same?
4. What does it mean to pray sensibly? Give some guidelines.
5. How does God want us to pray?
6. Discuss or list and reflect on reasons people sometimes give up on prayer.
7. List reasons we should persist in prayer and not give up. What is the importance of praying for the church?
8. Are all prayers answered one way or another? Explain your answer. How do you know when and if your prayer is answered?
9. Share what you have learned about prayer over the years.
10. Why is the element of trust an important aspect of prayer?

Activities

As a group: Exchange prayer requests with members of your group.

At home: Pray for members of your group this week, remembering their requests. Pray too for others, including family and friends.

Prayer: *Dear God, thank you for the gift of prayer. Help us remember that prayer is about developing a friendship with you over the years through daily conversations. May we remember the power of prayer and use it to help others and further your kingdom. Amen.*

Chapter 12: From Fear to Confidence: "The Name of God Is 'I Shall Be There' "

Snapshot Summary

This chapter uses the story of Moses to remind us that God is always with us.

Reflection/Discussion Questions

1. What lessons do we learn from the story about Moses at the burning bush?
2. Why is "I Shall Be There" an appropriate name for God?
3. What excuses did Moses give to God? What excuses have you made?
4. In what ways are you similar to Moses in your relationship with God?
5. Share a time when you faced a "Pharaoh" and felt the strength of God with you.
6. Who or what has helped you go from fear to confidence on your spiritual journey?

7. Share a time when you felt you were wandering, but found out that God was with you all along.
8. How does faith in God help you face the prospect of your own death or the deaths of loved ones?
9. Is fear or faith a better motivator? Explain your reasoning.
10. What key learning from this chapter will you most reflect on in your personal life today? This week?

Activities

As a group: Create a bookmark for your Bible with the words "I Shall Be There." Locate verses in the Bible that you feel demonstrate this promise.

At home: Remember and meditate on God's promise, "I Shall Be There," as you face any challenges this week.

Prayer: *Dear God, we are often like Moses. We give you excuses instead of our obedience. Remind us that faith conquers our fears and that you promise to be always with us. Amen.*

Chapter 13: From Not Knowing the Words to Knowing the Code Words of Faith: "The Windtalkers"

Snapshot Summary

This chapter explores the language of the Christian faith, including the key words of "incarnation," "grace," and "conversion."

Reflection/Discussion Questions

1. What important lessons are brought to mind by the story of Jephthah and the Ephraimites?

2. Why is "incarnation" a key word in our vocabulary of faith?

3. In your own words, explain the meaning of "grace," and discuss its importance.

4. What are some code words in your profession or vocation?

5. Explain why "conversion" is a key code word of faith.

6. How do we learn our key words of faith?

7. Who has helped you learn the significance of key words of faith?

8. How have faith words changed since the time of Jesus?

9. How do our key words of faith enhance our worship experience and our music?

10. What key learning from this chapter will you most reflect on in your personal life today? This week?

Activities

As a group: Ask each participant to write down two favorite words of faith, then briefly share why these words were chosen, and their importance.

At home: Reflect on the language of God. Speak the language of faith to God in prayer. Look for opportunities to use words of faith in daily conversation.

Prayer: *Dear God, thank you that you have given us our own special words to communicate with you. Our words of faith provide us with hope, life, and victory as we walk with you. Help us remember your love, and that you are always near. Amen.*

Chapter 14: From the Fear of Death to the Promise of Eternal Life: "What Do We Believe About Eternal Life?"

Snapshot Summary

This chapter explores what we believe about eternal life, why we believe it, and how faith conquers the fear of death.

Reflection/Discussion Questions

1. Why is it important to talk about death?
2. What death of a friend or family member had the biggest impact on you, and why?
3. Why do many people fear death? What do you think it is they fear about it?
4. How has your view of death changed or remained constant over the years?
5. Why do you believe in eternal life? Is it difficult or easy for you to imagine what heaven will be like? Explain your answer.
6. What lessons do we learn from the great Christians who did not fear death? What legacy do they leave us?
7. How does death contribute meaning to our lives? In what way is death a blessed servant?
8. Discuss or list and reflect on what Jesus taught us about life after death. What does it mean to you personally that "God is with us on both sides of the grave"?
9. How should death influence the way we live?
10. What passages in the Bible or other meaningful words have shaped your view of death and offered comfort in times of loss?

Activities

As a group: Use a hymnal or songbook to locate words and phrases of power and comfort concerning death and the promise of eternal life. Discuss or list and reflect on what hymns or songs offer you comfort in times of loss.

At home: This week, try to visit a cemetery or some other place of memorial to persons who no longer are here in physical presence. Reflect on the gift of life, and give thanks for the presence of God with us both now and in the life to come.

Prayer: *Dear God, thank you for this life and for your promise of eternal life to come. Help us as we struggle with our own mortality and the loss of family and friends. Remind us that you are with us always, and that death is not the end, but rather a new beginning with you. Amen.*

Chapter 15: From Trust in Self to Trust in God: "Can We Really Change?"

Snapshot Summary

This chapter looks at the elements needed in order for a turnaround to take place in our lives.

Reflection/Discussion Questions

1. In what way is trust related to change?
2. Why do we often trust self more than we trust God?
3. What's so difficult about change? List some of the usual obstacles.
4. It takes a certain amount of daring in order to change, the author says. Where does daring come

from? What makes us daring? Give an example from your life.

5. If you could snap your fingers and instantly change one thing about yourself, what would it be, and why?
6. When you attempt to change your behavior, what risks do you take?
7. Why is it important to have the desire to change? Where does desire originate? Can you change without having the desire to do so?
8. Share a time when you wanted to make a change in your life. What motivated you? Were you able to make the change? Why or why not?
9. Have you ever asked God's help to change? Why? What happened as a result?
10. How has this book and your reflections or discussions about its contents helped or challenged you?

Activities

As a group: Create your own *Turn Around* graduation certificates and sign them for one another with messages of love and encouragement.

At home: Reflect on your reading of this book and on this small-group experience. What lessons did you learn? What do you want to change? How will you begin?

Prayer: *Dear God, as our time together comes to a close, we remember what we have learned about new beginnings, and how you allow and empower turnarounds in life. Thank you for that. Be with us as we go out into the world and seek to do your will. Amen.*